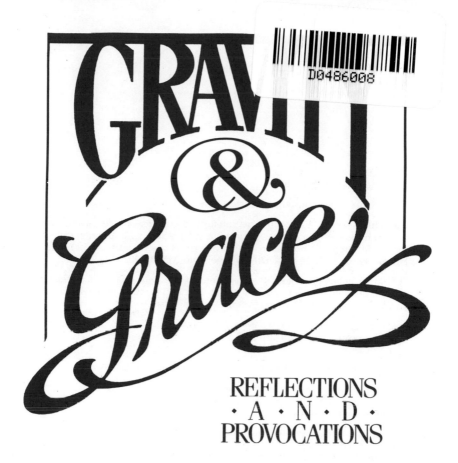

# GRAVITY & Grace

## REFLECTIONS · A · N · D · PROVOCATIONS

# Joseph Sittler

Edited by Linda-Marie Delloff
Foreword by Martin E. Marty

**AUGSBURG** Publishing House · Minneapolis

**GRAVITY AND GRACE**
**Reflections and Provocations**

**Library of Congress Cataloging-in-Publication Data**

Sittler, Joseph.
 GRAVITY AND GRACE.

 Includes bibliographical records.
 1. Theology—Addresses, essays, lectures. I. Delloff,
Linda-Marie.
BR85.S466  1986       230       86-3547
ISBN 0-8066-2205-9

Manufactured in the U.S.A.                    APH 10-2888

1   2   3   4   5   6   7   8   9   0   1   2   3   4   5   6   7   8   9

# Contents

# Foreword

The publisher and editor, but not the author, have asked me to introduce Joseph Sittler to new readers and to suggest to his devotees how to read this book. The author made no such request because *(a)* he sees no reason to make a fuss, and *(b)* if you asked him how to read it, he would say something like, "Well, you take it off the shelf. You open it. You use your eyes, proceeding from the upper left-hand corner to the lower right, line by line. Then you turn the page. . . ." Why should one need lessons in reading that rare theological work that is rare because it is so clear, so intelligible? Yet a book like this does merit some forewording, and those in charge asked me, and I enjoy the responsibility of passing it on with a few words.

First, recall that we imagined Sittler saying, "You use your eyes. . . ." On these pages the theologian lets slip what is a consuming complication of his life but for which he asks no pity: much of his eyesight (though none of his "vision") is gone. For many of us he remains

5

not only (in age) our sage, but (almost sightless) our seer. Yet he has had to accommodate with difficulty—and, I imagine and hope, not total grace—to the progressive loss of eyesight. And what use he made of those eyes! At a University of Chicago Divinity School luncheon where he addressed us as an *emeritus*, the host asked for questions. Students, who confide in Sittler as a senior pastor in their midst when they are one-on-one, were diffident, so the host turned to me. "Joe, if you had your full sight back for just one afternoon, what would you go to see?" I had not even reached the oral question mark when he shot back, "Chartres." Then he gave us a five-minute lecture on the glories of the blues in the cathedral windows there.

This book would not exist had not Paul A. Hanson and Shirley Teig of the American Lutheran Church Division for Life and Mission in the Congregation conceived the idea, and Linda-Marie Delloff, managing editor of *The Christian Century*, taken pains to select and edit excerpts from numerous lectures, papers, and conversations. What results is a surprisingly sustained set of discourses, but the selection can also be read chunk by chunk, paragraph by paragraph. The model is something like the *Penseés* of Pascal, or aphoristic writing in general. Modern literary critics and language philosophers like to debate what is the unit of discourse: the word, the sentence, the paragraph, the book, the life work? Sittler caresses his words and has devoured poetry in order to get words right. When people speak of his eloquence, they repeat various sentences which are natural-born epigraphs and aphorisms. Yet his prime unit is the paragraph. Each one has space and time for a triggering incident on which he reflects, a rehearsal of the reasons why he brings it up, and the reflection. Watch for examples.

Second, a how-to-read-Sittler manual has to say that he considers nothing he writes or says to be a finished product. The God of these pages is a God honored by humble traditions, but a God to be trusted—Sittler joins those who know not fully why—in regard to the future. Hans Urs von Balthazar has written that "resignation" may be a fine humanistic way of coping with physical decline, with aging, with life-toward-death, but it is not a particularly Christian virtue. Jesus, at least, embodies the forward look that we associate with youth and its adventure. Sittler, here as elsewhere, has spent too much energy reflecting on aging for us to dismiss his elegiac tone, his evocations of evening and autumn in life. Yet, however much he may protest youth cult and culture and refuse to see himself typed with it, there is something about his forward bent that should impel readers of these paragraphs to see him venturing to propose ways for their futures.

Sittler has trouble seeing ahead, literally and figuratively. Yet the natural man that he is cannot suppress this horizontal and venturesome way. Several summers ago we shared the platform at a large ministerial retreat. When his turn came, I would be called to read a Gerard Manley Hopkins poem, and then he, who knew it from memory anyhow, would exegete it for the group. Late in the week he let it be known that this would be his last such retreat or conference. His beloved Jeanne has been losing her health for years, and his devotion impels him to be close, just as his skill helps him to be of service. That plus the loss of most sight made travel difficult, made being away no fun.

In that context Sittler said, to an audience taking notes and recording tapes and even wiping tears, "No more. This is the last. Not only have I set this intention in concrete. I have done something more self-disciplining. I have told Jeanne that I won't go any more." Ten minutes later as we made our way back to our quarters, Joe asked: "What's the best way to fly to Kansas City? Flying is hard, but they say they need me there for an ecumenical gathering in Reformation and All Saints season." They need me there. I am sure that the Sittler family "covered" for Jeanne's missing spouse for a day or so, and that Kansas City made the flight feasible. I am also sure that here, as often, the hope side of Sittler's mind contradicted the memory side and won out. Watch how even the most reminiscence-filled paragraphs "lean forward" as it were. One needs lessons in such a thing, because so much theological and spiritual literature does not do that.

Which reminds me—and Sittler's paragraphs, like the man, are always reminders—of a third element to pass on to new readers, an element reinforced by a moment that summer. Someone asked Sittler what exactly he would counsel the church if it were to ask him how to go about reforming itself or being reformed. His ready answer was, "Watch your language!" He did not mean, as parents used to mean, that we should not be profane or obscene or violent. "Watch your language" meant and means, "take care" with your speech and writing. Language, which for him helps define not only the human but the divine-human connection, demands and deserves great attention. Had he the time he now gives Jeanne, the hours it takes to "hear" a book (which he still refers to as "reading"), and the sight to let him see the galleys, I am sure Sittler would be fussing and mess-

ing, seeking to get each line right. Yet despite his hand-
icaps, he is still serving the church by exemplifying what
he counsels. He watches his language, and wants us to
do the same.

This book contains surprisingly sullen and almost angry passages. Usually they are directed at the careless,
particularly if these have the care of souls and the priv-
ilege of communicating, against "flatulent" remarks by
clerics, and stupid ministers who do not read (and thus
they will never know they are being scolded here). At
the same time, there is a constant respect for the Christian congregation. I like the passage where he cites Karl
Barth. After 55 years of preaching Sittler learned not to
tell congregants how to live their lives. They are, most
of them, already doing better than the preacher, say
Barth and Sittler. Yet ministers who read this have no
reason to do so in a spirit of masochism. He honors their
profession and helps them "watch" to improve it.

I broke a self-imposed rule a paragraph ago by citing
Sittler's paragraphs. There is no point in doing that, for
it would challenge the integrity that Sittler displays
when he surprises. One is tempted to say "Watch for
this!" and "Watch for that!" in the spirit of the underpaid
and overeager tour guide. The sights along the way in
this book do not need pointers-out or exclaimers. They
take care of themselves. Watch, instead, for a sustained
effort to build on a trust in God that Sittler cannot account for, but which is his delight. Get to know his parents and others who have influenced him. "There's the
one about his mother and the Ziegfeld Follies. . . ." But
there I go again.

Watch, under it all, for the man his current seminary
colleagues and students call The Old Brooder brooding
about human limits, and the limitless bounty of God in

nature and grace. *Nature* and *grace:* these are the themes that Sittler would bring together, after "men" in his own and other Christian churches had rent them asunder. Watch for the way he displays what he talks about: a natural affirmation in a fallen world, and a grace that never lets itself be confined. For Sittler, grace is not something that forces smiles or induces arm-waving "Praise the Lords," though he would smile and pray. His grace is known so plausibly because this graceful thinker and speaker has also measured what is grave about life, and about his life. And so this book is the *Gravity and Grace* of Joseph Sittler, and of Sittler's God.

Pass it on.

MARTIN E. MARTY

# CHAPTER ONE

# Nature and Grace

Humankind has been here longer than my generation first supposed. Our history is yearly disclosed by research to be more and more complicated. But our existence on the earth as a small part of a single system of systems within systems that spin out into dreamlike magnitudes—this is the actual world of reflection in which the Christian faith must now ask after the relevance of its language. If we talk about creation, we mean more than the chrysanthemums and the bullfrogs and men and women. If we talk about redemption, we must ask if the ultimate meaning of redemption is confined to God's historical action for the human race in this place.

Theology is not only knowledge of human reflection about God; theology is also a constant doing, as well as a remembering, a transmitting, a refining. Theology is something that the church *does*, not only something that it *has*. Therefore a theologian is not simply a deep freeze in which the past is preserved and at certain times thawed out briefly for the attentive listener; theology is a vocation in which the accumulations of the past and the experiences of the present are always freshly attuned to the phenomena of the emerging, changing, frenetically racing world.

There are no logical, anthropological, psychological, or sociological definitions of *homo sapiens* in the Bible. But there are certain paradigms of where humanity stands. For example, in the very first chapter of the Old Testament there is a story in which human beings are spoken of from three angles of vision, as creatures with three dimensions, or as constituted by three enormous forces. First of all, we are from God. God is prior; he is the creator, we are the creatures. God calls us into existence. As Calvin used to put it, "Man's existence is a subsistence." We subsist under God's eternal existence. So our God relationship is the first building block of this structure.

God made the first human not out of angelic substance or out of sheer gas or wind, but out of the dust of the earth. This is a symbolic and powerful way of saying that the human race belongs to the biological order. We are part of nature. We cannot lay aside our natural beginning, our rootedness in the same ecological system that characterizes the natural world. That is both a psychological report and a theological report.

The main point of the story of Eve is not that God made a woman, but that he made another human being. For a solitary person has not the possibility of becoming a person. The human relationship of one person to another, person to neighbor, is a determining factor of personhood. This aspect of relationship, then, is the second element of the human structure.

And the third building block is that God put his creatures in the garden. God places, thrusts, his creatures,
roots them in nature. And the human relationship to
nature is such that we are to tend it. The garden, the
world of nature, is God's other creation, which stands
alongside his creation of persons, not as neutral or mute,
but as a living creation which has its own unique integrity and which defines the human place in the world.

Nature is never, for Jesus, simply a resource out of
which we are to dig iron and copper and zinc, and pump
oil; it is the theater of human life—the garden of our
life—which it is our obligation to care for.

You can't solve the whole problem of nature's care by
stewardship. That's a perfectly good word and a very
powerful idea, but it's not a big enough doctrine; it's not
central enough. For nothing less than the doctrine of
grace would be an adequate doctrine to shape the Christian community's mind and practice in a way appropriate
to the catastrophe in the environment.

God creates his creation in grace. The creation itself
is a realm of grace.

We must read the text very carefully: "The heavens
are telling the glory of God" (Ps. 19:1). But we must not
go on to say that the heavens disclose the will of God.
By going out on Sunday morning and looking up at the
heavens from the seventh tee, one has not performed
an adequate act of obedience. The will of God is not
disclosed via the heavens—though the glory of God,
according to the Scriptures, is.

Moralistic little essays here and there telling us to re-
cycle the newspapers and smash the cans (and we
should do both) are not sufficient efforts to care for our
environment. There must be some primary theological
reflection on this point.

What I am appealing for is an understanding of grace that has the magnitude of the doctrine of the Holy Trinity. The grace of God is not simply a holy hypodermic whereby my sins are forgiven. It is the whole giftedness of life, the wonder of life, which causes me to ask questions that transcend the moment.

I am interested in the reality or the presence of the grace of God in the creation, because only the doctrine of grace will be adequate to change the spirit of our minds whereby we deal with timber and oil, fish and animals, and the structure of cities, urban design, homes for people, places to work—all these mundane, concrete things that yet constitute the anchorage of our hearts, the home of our daily lives.

Nature is for enjoyment, in the profound meaning of enjoyment: to honor a thing for what it is, to consent to its being what it is and not another thing. Use nature, for sure, but use it only according to its inherent dignity.

\*

Contemporary humans are diminished because our roots are not as deep or as widely spread as were those of our forebears into the field, the forest, the woods. They do not touch the flowers, the animals, the daily tasks on the farm. Contemporary people, contemporary children particularly, think that hamburgers come from McDonalds. They think that Bordens makes milk and Kraft makes cheese. The closest any of them ever come to a lamb is a wool jacket. This increasing distance from the natural world has made our vocabulary bereft of natural images, has almost stripped us of the possibility to talk of ourselves in relation to God's creation.

In the course of history the human race has not only

sailed the seas but has pierced beyond its earth home-
land. Now it is piercing into the deepest recesses of
molecular life and cellular life. We are constituted by our
transactions with nature—not just the cattle on a thousand hills or the molecules under a thousand micro-
scopes. So deeply are we formed by our experiences of
nature that if the gospel is going to be addressed to
contemporary human beings, it's got to have a God who
follows those probings, a God of nature thus understood.

*

When we turn the attention of the church to a definition of the Christian relationship with the natural world, we are not stepping away from grave and
proper theological ideas; we are stepping right into the
middle of them. There is a deeply rooted, genuinely
Christian motivation for attention to God's creation, despite the fact that many church people consider ecology
to be a secular concern. "What does environmental pres-
ervation have to do with Jesus Christ and his church?"
they ask. They could not be more shallow or more
wrong.

Several years ago I attended three conferences relating
to this topic. The first was at Massachusetts Institute of
Technology, and it dealt with the obligation of the scientific community for the environment. Attending were
physical chemists, cosmographers, astrophysicists, physicists, agricultural experts, and others. The conference
was characterized by carefully written, data-rich, and
responsible papers on all aspects of the environment—
its present state, its fragility, what must be done to pre-
serve the ecological structure of our world.

At the end of the six-day meeting, a press conference

was called, and a small committee that had been as-
signed to prepare a summary statement came to a remarkable conclusion. They said, in substance, "There is
much that the scientific community can do, and much
more that we propose to do about the care of the environment. But no conceivable enhancement of research
methodology, no conceivable addition of public funds,
no cries of warning will make any considerable difference unless we are all changed in the spirit of our
minds."

I doubt if they knew they were quoting St. Paul in
that last phrase, which is extremely important. We must
not just change our minds. Minds are very fragile things;
we change them almost daily. But they said something
much more profound: we must be changed "in the spirit
of our minds." With our minds we *look* at things, but in
the spirit of our minds we *behold* things. The difference
here is not only linguistic. To look at a thing is what the
psychologists call an act of perception. To behold a thing
means to regard it in its particularity—its infinite pre-
ciousness, irreplaceability, and beauty. This statement
stimulated my thoughts on the problem of humanity
and the natural world.

Then I went to another conference, one held at the
University of Chicago and attended by teachers of the
country's leading law schools. The topic was: "What is
the role of public law in the care and protection of the
environment?" The lawyers presented serious papers,
but I read a news release at the end of it, and it was
uncannily like the one from the conference of scientists.
They said there is much that public law ought to do,
and will do, for the environment. No conceivable operation of public law by itself, however, will provide any
significant solution to human misuse of the earth. In

addition, they pointed out, the role of public law is important, but its pace is very slow. For there to be a law there must first be information. Then a consensus must be forged; then a law must be pushed through to legislation, and whereas the degradation of our environment is proceeding at a gallop, public law advances at a crawl.

The third conference I attended was by no means as prestigious as the first two. It wasn't really a conference, in fact; it was a meeting of some clergy on the same topic. During the meeting, a well-respected clergyman uttered this particularly foolish statement: "This is my Father's world, this is God's world. And if God wants us to take care of the world in a certain way, and we don't do it, then God will certainly, in his way, look after things no matter what we do." I thought that a very strange reading of the doctrine of God and the doctrine of nature. It reminded me of some wonderful passages in the Old Testament: "And God gave them what they wanted and made them sick of it," or, "God led them home by way of the wilderness." The reprisals of God's creation against its abuse may be slow and invisible for generations, but God is just. Sooner or later nature reacts against its exploitation.

In my own Lutheran tradition, the development of our theology, our hymnody, our liturgical language, our ordinary preaching almost never intersects the problems of the natural world. Why is that? This is, indeed, my Father's world. We sing the hymn, but we do not preach the substance, nor do we get it very often in our prayers or our liturgy. Why is that? This question has bothered me for a long time.

I think the reasons Lutheran theology and piety are not known for any specific or any analytically delicate feeling for the problems of the environment are several. First, we use the Old Testament in our praises and in our liturgical actions with right gratitude, but we have quite sharply misunderstood the first chapter of Genesis. "And God blessed them, and God said to them, 'Be fruitful and multiply, and fill the earth and subdue it; and have dominion over the fish of the sea and over the birds of the air and over every living thing that moves upon the earth' " (Gen. 1:28). The word *dominion* is a direct English effort to translate the Latin. In English *dominion* suggests *domination,* but that is an incorrect translation. The Hebrew statement is, rather, "And God said you are to exercise care over the earth and hold it in its proper place."

When one looks at that statement and considers the identity of the people to whom it was addressed, it makes considerable sense. The ancient Hebrews were surrounded by Canaanites who were nature worshipers, and God said to his chosen, "Nature is God's, but it is not God. Nature is not to be worshiped, but it is my gift, and you are to exercise care for my gift. You are to hold it in its proper place, and its proper place is very high."

In that same chapter is a discussion of the Garden of Eden. There is the root of the fact that when men and women want to express something that is the very profundity of their spirits, they reach for an analogy from nature: "Now is the winter of our discontent/Made glorious summer by this sun of York," or, "My love is like a red red rose." Why do I have to use the language of nature to serve the expanded understanding of my personhood? Because my personhood is of nature, natural but enspirited by the breath of the Creator. We have not taken enough account of the nature images in the Bible.

The second reason our Lutheran understanding of this matter is inadequate is the perverse side of one of our greatest virtues: our radical Christocentrism. That is, our theology is almost exclusively a theology of the Second Article. "I believe in God the Father Almighty, maker of heaven and earth" (Article One). "And in Jesus Christ, His only Son, our Lord" (Article Two). "And in the Holy Spirit, the Lord and giver of life" (Article Three). These three are ways of speaking of the activity and reality of one God. But we Lutherans have had a compulsive fascination with the Second Article. Jesus Christ, and him crucified, is the heart of Luther's, and hence our, theology.

In the 16th century, fundamental tilts and accents and statements of our theological tradition were given classical formation. In that century's Reformation, what was needed as over against the human authoritarianism, the sacramentalism, the sacerdotalism, and the monasticism of the church was a radical Christocentric doctrine. And Luther was tactically right in putting forth the idea, "Unless I be shown that this is the gospel of Christ, I buy nothing else."

Luther was tactically quite right, and he was biblically quite right. But to be right at a certain moment is not necessarily to be completely adequate for all time. Luther is not always utterly adequate to every situation.

It is important that we understand our Christocentrism at the point, as it were, at which God becomes historically present, radiant, incandescent, available for our knowing and historical reality. This is the doctrine of God in Christ. God was in Christ reconciling the world unto himself—but it is always God, God, God, in all three persons.

Against this background we must understand the doctrine of grace. Each person in the Holy Trinity points to and accents the reality and the activity of the one God. So we cannot say love belongs to God and grace belongs to Jesus.

We talk about the Old Testament in the same way. We often talk as if the God of the Old Testament were a God of law only; but then we go right ahead in our liturgy and use the Psalms, which have a magnificent rhetoric of grace. In sermons we keep on talking about the Old Testament being all law, but God is always a God of grace. The Hebrew word translated *charis* or grace in the New Testament, is *hesed* or *hen*, and these two Hebrew words can only be translated to mean that one lives under a God of grace. David knew that and died in that faith. Abraham knew it, as St. Paul and the letter to the Hebrews both testify.

The manger child was the incarnation of grace, not the inventor or the origin of grace. Thus, if grace characterizes the whole of Christian theology—God the Father, God the Son, and God the Holy Spirit—what does this mean for our understanding of the natural world?

Christian motivation comes out of discipleship: understanding the will and the purpose of God. This reluctant literature that some of the denominations are issuing on stewardship is not wrong, but it isn't very exciting either. What we need is to relate back to the first point: the change in the spirit of our minds must come about by putting the grace of God behind the eyes with which we look at the world and into the hands with which we touch the world.

And of course God's grace inheres in nature too. The early church fathers of the third and fourth centuries used two wonderful phrases that have almost fallen out of contemporary theology. They talked about "special grace" and "common grace." By "special grace" they meant that historical, incomparable appearance of the grace of God in Jesus Christ. But Augustine said that we were all born into the world of "common grace." *Common* does not mean low or moderate; it means available to everyone. By common grace the early church thinkers meant the grace into which everyone is born.

Before one is baptized, or even if one never is, such grace meets one in God's creation. There is a common grace in the pear tree that blooms and blushes. There is common grace in the sea (that massive cleanliness which we are proceeding to corrupt), in the fact that there was, before we laid hands on it, clean air. Our task is to appreciate that grace.

God's creations in the world are his voice, appealing to you and to me not only to join all people of good will in doing what intelligent things we ought to do about the creation, but one thing especially: to love the world and care for it to the glory of God.

\*

The land is against large-scale changes. Nature is what it is in its ecologically intricate structure because of the long time in which small modifications have occurred and were absorbed into the whole. Recently I was talking with an Iowa farmer about the way intensive land use has changed from what we knew in our youth. Farmers then had a grassy corner of the field where they

turned their horses and their plows, and later their trac-
tors, around. My farmer friend recalled that his father
taught him to call these unplowed margins "God's frame
around the picture."

Now farmers plow right up to the edges of the fence
or the ditch. As a result, what we used to call hedge-
rows—bushes or wild growth around the fields—have
been destroyed in large part. This means that the cover
for birds is taken away. And birds eat insects; they have
them for breakfast, lunch, and dinner.

We have destroyed a situation of natural predation
upon insects, and therefore we have to add more things
to the land, the plants, and the air to control the insects.
Nature is like a fine piece of cloth: you pull a thread
here, and it vibrates throughout the whole fabric.

*

A working, joyful relation to the land has spirited,
health-giving power. Around 1684 an old Puritan
preacher, William Davenport, said in a famous sermon,
"We have been dispatched by God and by history on
an errand into the wilderness to create, on this land, a
city on a hill, a light in the wilderness to all men." This
is a marvelous statement about the promise and hope
of the first people who came to this country. They came
to this fabulous continent for a fresh opportunity. In
some ways the American achievements have been great:
we have exercised the American characteristics of goodness of heart, hard work, ingenuity, and cooperative
adventurousness. Many good things have come out of
the American experience, but we have paid a high price
for them in the way we have assaulted the land. Our
errand into the wilderness has tempted us to forget the
message we were sent to deliver.

CHAPTER TWO

# *Faith: Trust and Risk*

The word *faith* is often misused. I remember a form that college students had to fill out. On it was the question, "What faith are you?" They meant Lutheran, Presbyterian, Methodist, or whatever. But Lutheranism is not a faith; it is a particular formation within the family of Christian believers with its own mores, liturgy, confessions. *Faith* must refer to something that is redemptive. A Lutheran church is not redemptive. It may be a servant of the message of redemption, but only God is the redeemer. *Faith* is a word that refers only to an object worthy of absolute trust. It is in God that one must have faith.

We have no access to Jesus. We have access only to the witnesses of the community that he called into existence by his presence, his person, his power. That is not disputable; that is a fact. I stand in a faith

23

relationship exactly where they stood. They had to believe in him—just as I do. They were no better off than I am, nor I than St. Peter, St. John, St. Thomas. John said, "We have beheld his glory, glory as of the only Son from the Father" (John 1:14). There is no proof of these things. The Christian community arose because its members believed Emmanuel; and they are the ones who reported to us indirectly.

All the theology of the church came later as a way to explicate and account for this reality. The fundamental records are a witness of faith to faith. We stand in the *continuity* of the faith, not of its demonstrable *certainty*. What is demanded of me is no less an act of faith than was demanded of Peter, Paul, or John.

To be a Christian is to sail on perilous seas. We live by faith, and it's never a finished faith. Mine has been collapsed and lying around me in shambles time after time. I've had to stop and reconsider and slowly build it up again, inasmuch as one builds it by oneself.

To build, we reinvestigate, see whether or not the new language can interpret more profoundly the old episodes and words. The task is never done. "I believe; help my unbelief!" (Mark 9:24). That's exactly where we all stand—even Luther, for example. Time and again in his own confessions, Luther talks about moments of what he calls *Anfechtungen*, when he had the horrible fear that he might have been wrong.

We resist the notion that the struggle toward the light is lifelong, but that is the fact.

\*

In recent years, there has been a clamorous demand in theological schools for teaching about spirituality—

an interest not characteristic of the Protestant tradition. Spirituality has been dealt with in a formal way mostly in Roman Catholic and Eastern Orthodox courses of study.

What is back of this sudden emergence of interest? One reason it is difficult to comprehend is that there are terms, as there are indeed realities to which the terms point, which are incapable of specification—for which we can have no definition of sufficient inclusiveness that it leaves no remainder. Some things I can define very precisely, but there are words in our language—indeed in every language—that elude definition. The word *imagination* is not capable of definition; yet we all know the word and recognize its referent when it appears. And the word *spirituality*—the power, presence, dynamics of the spirit—is not a definable reality.

We use the word *spirit* and we recognize the presence that it points to even in the secular use of the word. We talk about such a thing as an American spirit; but it is impossible to define that spirit in terms that are negotiable to someone not an American.

There is certainly such a thing as a French *esprit*. I saw it one day in a humble, but clear, manifestation. During a sabbatical year in Paris I was walking on the street in an old, very poor section of the city, a working people's section. And there came down the street on her way from school a little French girl whose shoes were broken-down and who was dressed in a frock that looked like it had been made from a sewed-up flour sack. She was poor, obviously, but she swung along the avenue with a flower stuck in her black hair and the grace of a princess, as if to say, "Here is a little French girl, and don't you forget it." There is a kind of *élan* in the French spirit that we are all aware of. But when we try to nail the word down, we're in trouble.

In another usage of the word Isaiah said, "The Spirit of the Lord God is upon me" (Isa. 61:1). The Spirit of God is something I cannot define, much less enclose. We so often think of that Spirit as a generally dispersed and gaseous holy presence. It is simply there. We breathe it in, we breathe it out. There is a sense in which the Spirit inheres in all things. There is a sense in which the Spirit of God is simply a wide term for the creative presence of God in everything that God has made.

But note the text, "The Spirit of the Lord God is upon me, because the Lord has anointed me to bring good tidings to the afflicted; . . . to proclaim liberty to the captives." May I suggest with some boldness of interpretation that the Spirit gains specificity in relation to a focal duty, that the Spirit is given with a task. In New Testament times lepers had to be pronounced clean by a priest before they could be readmitted to society. When Jesus told ten lepers crying to him from afar to go show themselves to the priests, he was absurdly promising them that they would no longer be leprous. Yet despite the absurdity of the command and the promise, we read this wonderful sentence: "And as they went, they were cleansed" (Luke 17:14). They did not receive the gift and then take off; they took off in obedience, and the gift was given in relation to the obedience.

The gift of the Spirit is not just a vaporous cloud of unknowing, but the gift is given when obedience is demonstrated. The assignment of a task is the occasion for the specificity of the Spirit; the precision of the gift is accommodated to the acceptance of a duty.

When I was ordained to the ministry, I really didn't feel any particular inbreathing of the Spirit, nor had I ever regarded myself as a very spiritual person (nor do I still so regard myself). But, as my father assured me when I observed that some of my fellow students seemed to have a sure and certain call to the ministry, "There are certain things you can do if you will, and there are certainly those very things that you can do that need doing. How loud do you want it to speak?" In other words, to quote a line from Theodore Roethke's poem, "The Waking": "I wake to sleep, and take my waking slow./I learn by going where I have to go."

When we take on the job, the Spirit is given in relationship to the obedience. The Spirit of the Lord God is upon me because he sent me.

St. Augustine, at the beginning of his *Confessions*, makes a great and beautiful statement: "Thou has made us for thyself, O Lord, and our hearts are restless until they rest in thee." Back of that statement lies a proposition which says that the human is created for transcendence. It is the Jewish and Christian belief that we are meant for a selfhood that is more than our own selves—that we are by nature created to envision more than we can accomplish, to long for that which is beyond our possibilities.

We are formed for God; we are formed to be in relation to that which was before we were, from which we proceed, and in which we will ultimately end. Faith is a longing. Humankind is created to grasp more than we can grab, to probe for more than we can ever handle or manage.

This transcendental restlessness has two parts. First, I cannot unfold, in the totality of my possibility, to the level of that which I dream. Second, the one who placed the dream in me is the Creator. We are made in the image of God. We are made after the image and the likeness of the ultimate thing itself. Our whole life is an effort to approach, to appreciate, to some degree to participate in, the absoluteness of God himself. But we can never do it; that's why our whole life is a restlessness.

This restlessness may make us want to throw in the towel—or to pull up our socks. You can play it either way. You can either be creatively restless, as before the unknowable, or you can simply collapse into futility. One of the goals of the Christian message is to join together the people of the way, the way of an eternally given restlessness, and to win from that restlessness the participation in God, which is all that our mortality can deliver.

When we Americans think of the word *equip*, we conjure up certain images. I am a teacher; I have certain equipment—mainly books—which I must use to do my work. Many years ago I had a little fight with the Internal Revenue Service. I bought the *Oxford English Dictionary*. Every single word in the English language is there, given its meaning with illustrations from English literature starting in Chaucer's time and continuing up to the present. It's a magnificent piece of work, and it cost at that time, secondhand, $300. I deducted it from my income tax under the law that a workman may deduct the cost of his tools (such deductions are now common).

I was called downtown, where a young man behind a desk seemed to have a particularly fussy interpretation of that law: "What's this? You bought a bunch of books costing $300. You can't deduct books under the meaning of that law."

So I said, "Well, why not? If I were a plumber, you would expect me to deduct the cost of wrenches and threaders and elbows. I'm a teacher; words are my business. They're the only tools I have. And if I'm going to do it right, I've got to have the best dictionary I can get."

I'll never forget the astonishment with which he said, "You know, you almost sold me."

"Well," I said, "I want to sell you completely."

He grew tired of my argument, I guess, because he finally said, "Get out of here. It's OK."

We think of equipment as that which we need to do the thing we want or ought or are called to do. However, that is only half the use of the word. If we think of equipment that way, we're thinking of something added on to ourselves. Equipment—*katartismos* in Greek—is also used to mean an internal nurture, an internal formation that matures one's competence for an appointed task. To equip the saints refers in part to certain things that God's followers must add to themselves, as in the great passage, "Stand therefore, having girded your loins with truth, and having put on the breastplate of righteousness" (Eph. 6:14). These are equipments provided by the Lord of the church, by the faith. But the other meaning of the word says to nurture; that is, to cultivate. *Katartizo* is also used in the letter to the Hebrews—inwardly to fulfill: "Now may the God of peace who brought again from the dead our Lord Jesus, the great shepherd of the sheep, by the blood of the eternal covenant, equip you with everything good that you may do his will, working in you that which is pleasing in his sight, through Jesus Christ; to whom be glory for ever and ever. Amen" (Heb. 13:20-21).

Just who are these saints? Here again is a word that has become almost stylized by 1500 years of Roman Catholic usage. In the New Testament, "the saints" refers to those who have heard and obeyed, who have had their lives inwardly transformed by what they have heard and believed in the community of faith. Luther has a wonderful sentence about the saints: "To be a saint is to be a forgiven sinner."

In the Roman Catholic hagiography the saints are those who are very special, whose gifts of grace or whose achievements of courage or gallantry, up to the point of martyrdom, have been so esteemed by the church that they have been singled out. But in Luther's sense, saints are forgiven sinners. All Saints' Day is the day when we remember the dead who have preceded us in the great stadium of the church—the "great cloud of witnesses." You and I are saints. In the New Testament sense we are part of the *laos,* the people of God. To equip these sorts of saints does not mean to provide people with exterior additions to their sainthood or to their witness, to their fidelity or their personality, which will somehow be like shoulder pads and helmets. Instead, it means to equip in the internal sense: not an adding-on-to, but a maturation, nurturing, deepening, opening of vision, growing in faith.

In the internal processes of faith, the word *equip* has some relationship to the word *order.* You order your library so you don't have to look through all your books to find the one you want. Or one orders the shop, or the bench, or the office—whatever kind of place he or she works in. Each person has individual ways of doing this. There are a thousand ways to order things, and only the individual knows what is the right order for him or her; what is order to one person may look like a spattered chaos to another.

I had an aunt who saved boxes. She had to save boxes in order to contain all the other things she saved, and she ordered them with magnificent clarity. The big boxes were all together, regardless of what they held. The little boxes were all together, regardless of what they held. One of the funniest things I ever saw in my life was a little box labeled "pieces of string too short to save." This was order appropriate to the New England mind that never threw anything away.

Order has an interior dimension. One orders one's life according to an intention or a purpose. Fundamentally, we must order ourselves to bring to our lives integrity, which is related to the word *integer,* which means unity in Latin. The number one is an integer. It suggests being a harmonious person, an integral person, one who knows where the center is and who works out of that center. This is what it means to have an orderly life of faith, to be equipped as a saint.

Each person's pilgrimage into a profounder spiritu- ality is a highly personal matter. One's way of prob- ing for depth will be congruent with his or her whole nature. One cannot lay out programs for spirituality. But while spirituality may be personal, it is not individual. There are ways of deepening one's spiritual reflective life that have a universality beyond individual experience.

The concept of order occurs in the Scripture many times. On the first page, we have a cosmos and not a chaos; God created a cosmos by ordering. The biblical literature often marvels at the stars, the moon, and the sun. One of the most common themes in all human reflection is amazement at the fabulous order which characterizes the world: the periodicity of sun and moon and stars, the turning of the seasons.

Human historical life both envisions and longs for an ordering whereby chaos shall be brought into such form as to make an integral personal life, not just a spattering of experience. This longing for order is not just a house-keeping fussiness within the mind; it is a deep thrust within the spirit.

Not only is there a deep human longing for order; there is a command for it. "I am the Lord your God, . . . you shall have no other gods before me" (Deut. 5:6-7). That admonition means that oneness is a focal point which orders the whole chaos. Life is a graduated series of evaluations, doxologies, attestations. I have many interests, concerns, foibles, attitudes. But I must obey that commandment, not only because it is God's commandment but because the structure of life and my own nature demand that I cannot live in disorder. God is the name of the ultimate order. "Seek first the kingdom of God," or to change that into ordinary speech: "Seek first a kingly rule within your life, and all these other things shall be put in their place," said our Lord.

What I am calling spirituality or inwardness cannot be matured by programming. There are helps, there are models, but one cannot teach this kind of thing. One can only speak of occasions when this quality emerges. Look at its indubitable appearance here and here and here, and ask, "By what series of events, by what kind of reflection did this order come to be?" Then translate that into your own life experiences. Here is an example from my experience.

Some years ago I was a member of a group of about 20 who used to meet for discussions. Once we gathered in New Orleans at the home of a Roman Catholic female order. The room for our meeting was down a long hall, and halfway down that hall was the chapel. Every morning as I went down to our meeting, every noon as I went back to my room, early afternoon after lunch when we reassembled, and in the evening, I noticed that the sisters, about 30 of them, were sitting there in that chapel.

There was an absolute silence. They were simply there, four times a day, apparently for a period of 15 minutes of prayer and meditation. That made me reflect, coming from the much-speaking community of the Lutheran church. I noticed that there in the chapel, there was no leader. In the front of the chapel and over the altar was, of course, a large crucifix. And at that moment I began to wonder, is there any other image in the history of the world that could survive such constant gazing, reflection, and prayer? What other form could absorb all of the worries and apprehensions heaped upon it? Is there any other image in the world that could stand the weight of so profound a demand? And the answer was immediate and obvious: no.

What is it about the figure of the crucified God that has enabled generation after generation, century after century, to sustain so great a weight of human woe? I began to probe and push at the question, and have continued to do so over the years. Why is it possible that from the earliest remains we have of the Christian community, through the great medieval period, into the Reformation, into today's world, the figure of the crucified one upon the cross has been the center of devotional gravity, the center of human pain and torment?

Unless the God before whom we sit, and at whom we gaze, and about whom we think—unless that God has the tormented shape of our human existence, he isn't God enough. We ask, "Why did God become human?" And the answer is that the God who wants to be the source of our order must become the horror of our disorder, or he has no authority.

A marvelous message of the Christian faith is that the eternal order became our disorder and died of it; therefore, he has the right to say, "I am the Lord."

To push a problem in this way until you get some kind of a clarification is one way to grow in depth. Order demands discipline. This need not be a coercive or programmed discipline whereby everybody does the same thing at the same time. But discipline there must be: the discipline of the Roman Catholic sisters; the discipline, before Vatican II at least, of the Roman Catholic priests. You would see them on trains, on buses, with their little zipper-closed, black prayer books or missals, reading every day, as they were obliged to do in the course of the week, all the Psalms. No matter where they were, they'd take out their missal book and read that day's complement. Often it must have been automatic, but the language sinks in. The images percolate. The notions of the language bypass cerebral operations and become part of the organism. The mode whereby order is invited and achieved is not decisive; that discipline and order belong to God is decisive.

We are tempted to regard God primarily as a God for solitude and privacy and only secondarily as a God for society. We have a God for my personal ache and hurt, but no God for the problems of human life in the great world. This is where the church has tended to be privatistic, solitary, filled with religious sentiment of a personal kind. We need not abolish that aspect, but it should not have undue importance. We must expand our doctrine of God to acknowledge that he is not only the Lord to whom I flee in times of trouble, but he is also the maker of heaven and earth—God of all that is.

When we say, "I believe in the Holy Spirit, the Lord and giver of life," the reference is not just to religious life, devotional life, prayer-book life. It means all of life.

The old shape of the confirmation order is now radically inappropriate in its structure; in its culturally formed past it is not adequate to our present circumstances. The culture that formed the order was heavily rural. Most formal education ended with the completion of elementary school. The youth at that school would leave to begin engagements with farms or mills or stores. Hence the age of 13 or 14 seemed an appropriate time for a course of religious instruction to wind up. But now in new circumstances, why could we not be theologically inventive and create a fresh rite for that significant moment in the unfolding and maturation of young life? Many people would regard this as being bold beyond what the church ought to do. But the church has always been inventive. Religious faith is not a dull plodding; at its best it is characterized by a soaring inventiveness. However, it seems to me that today we are often too cautious to be creative.

\*

There are still voices abroad today that have the effrontery to suggest that only infallible, inerrant literalism is the Christian way to interpret Scripture. This proposing of a highly peculiar norm for the whole of world Christianity is a strange phenomenon. We ought not to fall for it.

On the first page of the Bible there is an instance of how literalism is but an invitation to transcend the image to which literalism points. That first page is not geology, biology, or paleontology; it is high religion. For there we are told who we are in terms of our constitutive context. And if we could understand that, we would cease worrying about whether the antelopes or the cantaloupes came in a certain order.

\*

The adoration of God begins not with Christ, but with the one who made heaven and earth. Jesus never called himself Messiah. He did not claim to be God. He claimed to be of God, from God. But he did not claim to be God.

There are different ways of talking about God. The phrase "son of God" is used in the Old Testament for persons of whom there is no claim of divinity. That is, the term "son of God" is not a biological reference. God

is not a biological datum. God does not beget sons as
we do. The term "son of God" is a metaphor.

For example, Thomas was a Jew. By virtue of being a
Jew he would never call anyone else God, an unspeak-
able word to a Jew. When he called Jesus "My Lord and
my God," he meant, "That which I understand by the
word *God* is certainly here, and this one represents it,
or he is the personal presence of it."

But the notion of having an ontological identity, being
of one substance, is otherwise. Look at the language of
the Nicene Creed. It does not say "one substance," but
it says "being of one substance." The word in Greek is
*ek*—"God from God, light from light, true God from true
God." The ancient writers carefully avoided making an
absolute identity. At the same time they denied a chasm
in reality between the two. The reality of God meets us
in the reality of Jesus. That's a different statement from
saying God and Jesus are an identity.

*

Even our love, even our generosity, even our self-
giving to another, is characterized by a horizontal
negation across the positive of love. This becomes ter-
rifyingly clear when we think about our own piety and
devotion.

In response to the Lord's command I say my prayers.
And when I pray, I am happy that I am doing it. Then
I reflect on the happiness I feel, the purity and goodness
I feel in being in an act of prayer, and I immediately
begin to congratulate myself because I am doing it. And
then I think, "That's not right." I then reflect what a
really fine fellow I am after all, because I have the sen-
sitivity to be aware that I ought not so to congratulate

myself. I have succeeded only in raising my self-righ-
teousness to a new level.

And then I think next, "That isn't right." But if I know
it isn't right, then I also am relieved in part from the
guilt, because I know it isn't right.

And the whole interior life goes round and round and
round, with deepening ambiguities, which are the bur-
den of being human.

Now this perception of the internal life in its limita-
tions, in its ambiguity, in its egocentricity—this is the
human situation. Therefore, God has come to me
through that great sign of himself, that condensation of
the reality of God, which is the suffering one on the
cross. God has to come to me in that way if he's going
to be a God who really takes the measure of my heart.
If he's going to be what we are in order that we might
be reconciled with what he is, he's got to become nothing
less than both the promise and the awesome ambiguity
of our human life. The interior crossings of myself at
prayer are met by God, who comes to me on a cross.

The affirmation of faith is not a pure leap into the
unknown; one can also have "reasons" for believing, although all reasons are not negotiable or provable.
I think the word *certainty* will perhaps have to disappear
from the Christian vocabulary—not because our ances-
tors didn't mean something clear by it, but because the
word has by now been permeated with positivism.

I think it's true to say that most of us want what the
term pointed to. That is the great appeal of Pentecos-
talism; its adherents invite you to join the idolatry of

provable fact. And if it's really that way, then you don't need faith.

✳

Faith is a word that connects hope and God. As Luther put it, "Faith is trust." And then he added another sentence that is so shocking I rarely hear it quoted. He said "By faith I mean a trust in God's unknown, unfelt, untried goodness and mercy." God is ultimately unknowable. And faith in God is built on precisely his unknowable qualities.

✳

Our Christology is terribly threatened these days by making it into a Jesusology. Jesus is always the presence, the force, the invitatory incarnation of God.

Once at a church where I was interim pastor for a year, there was a woman really hooked on the "me and Jesus" movement, and she used prayer as a kind of personal lubricant to everything she wanted. She worked at a hospital in Chicago, and she used to tell me, "Every morning when I drive from my house to the hospital, I pray to Jesus that he will find me a parking spot. And you know, pastor, he always does." I kept asking myself, "What kind of God-relationship is built on this parking-space-finding Jesus that will sustain this woman in profound deprivation and tragedy? Is it enough?"

One Sunday morning I said to her, "Emma, suppose there is another woman driving in the second lane on the highway taking a sick child to the hospital, and you drive right in to the parking space that Jesus found for you, and this woman who is frantic with a sick child can't find a space. How about her?"

"She didn't pray hard enough," was her retort.

That really stumped me. So I tried to think of how to correct her, but she was immune to argument.

Well, finally I found one, and I am sinfully proud of it; I think it was a straight gift. The next time I saw her I said, "You know this speech you give me about Jesus finding you a parking space, Emma. What do you suppose Mary was praying about jogging along on that donkey on her way to Bethlehem?" Emma never mentioned the topic again. If Mary couldn't find a parking space in which to have a baby, particularly *that* baby, then there must be something wrong with the parking-space-finding Jesus.

✳

Sin is an unused, unfashionable word, but the facts of life (including my own life) as I look at them— the betrayals, the forgetfulness, the selfishness, the egocentricity—are but the history of humankind written small. There is only one answer to such a vision: it must be accepted. I must simply turn it over to nothing short of grace.

This exposure of the ever-deepening congruity between the mad parables of Jesus, the craziness of the gospel, the incomprehensibility of judgment and grace is the only pattern that seems not to anesthetize, not to cosmetize, the human reality. It seems the only pattern big enough to disclose the raw skeleton of human experience. I cannot prove the truth of the Christian faith, but I cannot escape the haunting congruity between the

doctrine of God and grace and love and sin and judgment. The more absurd the human drama becomes, the
more appropriate the divine drama discloses itself to be.

Growth in the life of the mind, a lifelong deepening
of reflection, may sometimes begin in awkward hesitation—or, equally, in the examination of snappy opin-
ions. If I continue throughout my life to regard with
ever-renewed admiration a Rembrandt self-portrait, my
mind is not enriched by ever more vehement statements
of my admiration. One must, rather, keep pushing the
question, "What is admirable about the admirable?" We
really do not get to know one another by exchanging
catalogs of our likes and dislikes. Real understanding
grows with probing.

When one is aware of a hesitation, everything hangs
on probing that hesitation. For example, I have never
found it possible to include mission to the Jews under
the general mission command to the church. As Paul
says, "God has not rejected his people whom he fore-
knew" (Rom. 11:2).

Incessant probing of that moment of hesitation has
for me produced a profound deepening in my understanding of Judaism, of the meaning of the law and of
the relation of the grace of God given in the law's guidance to God's ancient people, and that grace as actual-
ized and made present in the event of Jesus.

CHAPTER THREE

# The Word of God

Interestingly, no writer of antiquity whom I know anything about ever said, "There is neither male nor female" (Gal. 3:28). Aristotle didn't say it; Socrates didn't say it; Plato didn't say it; Solon, the Greek legal authority, didn't say it. Nobody in the antique world until St. Paul ever expressed such a concept of an absolute erasure of sexual differences.

We humans are made for each other. The meaning of the Adam and Eve story, in particular the introduction of the figure of Eve, is not simply to say that it takes two to tango. But the Eve story communicates to all of us the meaning of the German proverb, "Ein Mensch ist kein Mensch." A solitary person is no person; personhood is relation and presupposes another for its actualization. God made a helpmate for Adam. Helpmate doesn't mean a sublieutenant; it simply means that which is necessary for wholeness. On this point, Scripture is very clear—and unique—in its perspective.

✻

Who is God? Scripture does not answer the question. It's a rather shocking thing to recognize, but Scripture at no point defines God. Rather, it says, "I am the holy one, I am the one who led you through the great and terrible wilderness, delivered you from captivity, called you by your name, made you a people, constituted you an elect nation, a holy priesthood." Or, "I am the one who before the mountains were brought forth, I was. Whatever happened, I did." God in Scripture is not the one who *is* but the one who *does*. This is a functional definition of God, not a dictionary definition.

Scripture never makes any effort to prove God's existence. Further, we do not know who Jesus was from his own statements. Jesus never said, "My relation to God is as follows," or, "My own internal religious feeling is as follows." Jesus never disclosed his interior self; we cannot probe into his psychology. As is true of God, we know who Jesus was only by what he did. We cannot give a definition of Jesus. The only access we have to him is through the reported word about him, and that word is not consistent. A single parable may be given this way in Mark and quite another way in Matthew or Luke. This means that theologically we have to build up the composite of differences, and then try to ask what the church—which knew these differences quite well—meant when it said, "Jesus is Lord."

✻

The Word became flesh and dwelt among us" (John 1:14). What do we mean when we refer to the Word of God? Primarily we do not mean Scripture; there was a Word of God before there was any Bible. The Hebrew term for word, *davar*, does not primarily mean something we say or write; it means that the creative force of God himself goes out of himself to do something.

There developed a body of literature written by a people who had been made a people by that force, and their writings are called the Word of God. The ultimate meaning of Word is not a document; but the documents were preserved by the ancient Hebrews and the early church because they testified, they bore witness, to the force of the Word. The people had experienced it, and they were transformed by it.

\*

Luther declared that the mother who teaches the child about the goodness of God, who is the shepherd of all children, is as much a doctor of the Word of God as is the archbishop of Mainz. So when the preacher preaches on "the Word of God," he or she might not quote Scripture. When one declares the presence and the grace of God, the Word is being preached. During the 10th to the 12th centuries, when virtually no one could read, how did the church continue? The people didn't read Scripture; in fact, many priests didn't either. So they didn't preach Scripture. What they taught was the celebrative worship of God through images and liturgy, hymnody, acts of devotion and tradition. So the church lasted without Scripture.

\*

I've preached on the parables for 55 years now, and I'm sure that I haven't reached the bottom; in fact, I've begun to doubt that there is a bottom. Every generation reads those parables over and over again in terms of its own questions, and in every case the freshness, the shock of Jesus' teaching, rocks us over and over again. There have been at least 10 new books on the parables in the past 2 or 3 years; why is that? Not because the parables have to be put into modern English. No matter what kind of English they are in, you can't reduce their puzzling depth.

Take the old Jewish father, reared traditionally, who does what was an incredible thing in a Jewish family: he runs down the road to meet his son who had demanded his part of the boodle and gone off. And now the son comes, full of pot as it were, up the road; and the old Jewish father does a shocking thing that reversed the traditional reverential distance between father and son. He leaves the religious dignity of his role as head of the family, and rushes down the road. He seizes the child and calls over his shoulder, "Put on a roast. Get him a ring for his finger and a garment."

Every Jew who read that said, "Come on, that's no way for a Jewish father to behave."

But that's exactly the way Jesus wanted it. He said, "No, that isn't the way it is in life; but I'm talking about the kingdom of God, not about the kingdom of Judea. Cherish your discomfiture."

Do not therefore read the parables as slick little stories of the ordinary; read them rather as they turn the ordinary upside down.

✱

In my experience so many things from biblical speech have entered into the materials of daily life, into reflective possibilities, that I'm not aware they were ever matters of conscious reflection. Time and again phrases come back when you need them, because they were put there before you ever thought you would need them, and they simply got stuck. I once went to a baseball game in New York with Franklin Clark Fry, who loved the New York Yankees next to the Lord, I think. Fry had been brought up, as I had, under a preacher father, and we were both soaked in the Scriptures.

In the ball game, Luis Aparicio, the famous Chicago White Sox shortstop who seldom made an error, did so. "Who can understand his errors?" quipped Fry. Another time, sitting in a meeting of the Ohio synod with Fry before he became president of the United Lutheran Church, a particularly puffy, pontifical character was making a flatulent speech, holding forth much too long, and Fry, quoting the psalm said, "Oh, Lord, we have sinnéd against thee."

These amusing reflections do not, I trust, divert too much from my point. The ancient vigor, color, sonority of the language of Scripture has a kind of stickiness to the memory. Phrases may remain like forgotten deposits in an account; but they are there for resurrection.

Scripture no longer has an automatic, revered, venerated authority simply because it is Scripture. There was a time when the biblical episodes, stories, and admonitions had an instantaneous and autonomous force because they were in a venerated, traditional book. For almost the whole of Western culture, that time has disappeared. If the authority of the biblical Word is no longer traditionally and generally accepted, or if the authority of the biblical Word is not any longer enthralled in commanding institutions like the church, but is, rather, freewheeling, then the authority we have to appeal to is intrinsically different.

The authority of scriptural words and passages is internal, not external, and it is not automatic. The authority of Scripture has to depend on the text's internal congruity with the human pathos: the reality of what it means to be a human being in this appalling time. The pathos, confusion, ambiguity, and scatteredness of life—this is the situation to which we must address the biblical Word. And that Word will be invested with authority by virtue of its liberating, enlightening, and promising congruity, not by virtue of "the Bible says." For most people, what "the Bible says" is no more authoritative than what the *New York Times* or the *Washington Post* says. The authority must be uncovered as intrinsic.

What is the difference between power and authority? Many exercises of power have no authority. And there are exercises of authority that do their work without power. Richard Nixon had the power of the presidency—up to the moment he resigned. But after the disclosures of his role in Watergate he had no authority.

On the other hand, Abraham Lincoln never used, except in a few instances, the full power of the presidency; but he had authority. He didn't have to use sheer power. Pius XII, the pope who preceded John XXIII, had and used the full power of the papacy. John XXIII never used the full outer power of the papacy, but he had enormous authority.

What is the difference? Authority is a force continuous with the whole nature and performance of the person or thing possessing it. My grandmother had authority; my grandfather had power. I remember what my grandmother said, and I wanted to do it. I have no remembrance of anything my grandfather said, except that I had to do it.

Scripture has both authority and power. It has great strength, but, most important, we want to do what it commands. That is its authority.

Deal gently with some things in Scripture, and don't think you have to crack every obscure reference. It has taken 300 years to write a fairly accurate commentary on Shakespeare's language, and there are some facts that were part of current history in Lancaster or York that are simply gone. We don't know what Shakespeare referred to. Why should we not think that Scripture, written much earlier, contains some passages that are, and probably will remain, unclear?

## CHAPTER FOUR

# Ministry:
# The Stewardship
# of the Mystery

The principal work of the ordained ministry is reflection: cultivation of one's penetration into the depth of the Word so that the witness shall be poignant and strong. Clergy have a particular responsibility to the discipline of the reflective life. But they are often negligent in this obligation. It's a terrible temptation to have one's life chopped up by what they tend to call administration, and the temptation must be resisted mightily so as to allow time for the real work of the job.

The contemporary church makes such demands on the minister that the poor individual must sometimes fight for his or her life. Those demands are for a series of virtues and activities that, compressed into one person, constitute an impossibility. One difficulty is in the area of education. If one is going to remain decently familiar with what is needed as a young professional scholar (I don't mean a research scholar), one must be like a good doctor. Most doctors don't do research, but they read the journals that keep them abreast of the research going on.

Most pastors will not do biblical or theological research, nor are they expected to. But most of them don't do what a good doctor does: subscribe to journals, take time to read, engage in programs of study whereby they keep abreast of information necessary to be professionally decent.

Sometimes when I go to a 25th anniversary of an ordination, or a church anniversary, I spend a few hours with the pastor in his or her study. I often see there the Levitical rule books that the student took away upon seminary graduation 25 years ago. But I see no evidence on the coffee table that the literature the pastor attends to is other than the most general reading of the American family. I find this very depressing.

A good teacher teaches her heart out trying to educate people about the excitement of biblical study or archaeology, for example, and then she finds that her students stash it all away and go out and preach sermons that are rich in piety and oversimplification—and the people love it.

✳

At a conference of pastors, I sat for two and a half days with a colleague at my side who presented some beautiful, clear, and fresh New Testament studies; he was a complete master of contemporary New Testament scholarship. I was to follow with a theological reflection. We worked very hard.

But while I was at breakfast, lunch, and dinner with these 120-some pastors, never did the conversation turn to what the two of us had been talking about. My colleague was introducing some astounding insights, and I was not exactly unexcited either. But here these pastors sat at meals three times a day and talked about how the walleyes were biting and they were going to have to get a new outboard and their old boat was bad; they would have to put a new roof on their cottage, and the building program at the church was $10,000 behind schedule. Not a blasted word for two and a half days about the topic of that conference.

If I were to attend a professional meeting of gastroenterologists, I'd expect doctors to be there to learn what is going on in that field. At that pastors' conference, the pastors should have been interested in new developments in their professional field.

On the whole I find many pastors dull and soggy in the brain—and I do not apologize for that statement. Ministers are often dull functionaries. Ordination was their intellectual stopping place.

I was once asked to preach an ordination sermon for a favorite student. As I prepared, I wanted to avoid all past ways of talking about ordination, because many of them I thought were clichés, worn so thin by frequent usage that they slid through the mind like a gelatinous substance on a floor without a rug. I kept looking at the formula for ordination and thinking, "What in keeping the question going is the particular, nonshared, nonsharable, absolutely specific job of this person? Why are we ordaining him to something that is not the same as

being a faithful, baptized child of God in Christ's church?
What's he got that the rest of us haven't got?"

My questions led me further to ask what actually constitutes the church. It is constituted by two things that
do not come out of history, society, human religion,
philosophical reflection on ultimate issues, or any human desire or intention. Those two things are Word and
sacrament: the gospel as it is transmitted, and the gospel
as it is celebrated in the dominical sacraments of the
Lord's Supper and Baptism.

The ordained ones—priests, pastors or ministers—
also cannot be other than that which constitutes the
church. Therefore I arrived at this conclusion: the ordained ones are the tellers of that story without which
the church was not, is not, and cannot continue. They
are those who tell the story of those events, promises,
and mighty deeds of God that constitute the church.

But cannot others tell the story? The church must keep
its story going and assure that there will never be a time
or place where the sacraments commanded by Christ
are not proffered. Therefore the church insists on pre-
paring a designated cadre to see to it that the constitutive
story is told, and that the nurturing sacraments are administered.

This is a way of defining the ordained pastorate of the
church that does not elevate it above the laity, but gives
it a particular job among the people of God.

\*

The notion that everybody has an equal right to authority on all matters is wrong—plain irrational. If
I go to graduate school for three years, my judgment on
relevant matters should be given a certain weight. My

views need not always prevail, but they must be heard. That's my job. I do not have the same right to write a prescription for my dog's bellyache that the animal doctor has, and I can't tell the man who comes in to fix the fireplace how to do it. But I don't think that's any denigration of the people of God.

There are varieties of gifts; and the ordained one is supposed to have been chosen by the church, or at least certified by the church, as having a set of gifts, and he or she must exercise these, while at the same time realizing their limits.

For reasons of good order, an ordained minister presides at the Eucharist. But we must not make a theological principle out of a provision for good order. My father, trained in the Joint (Lutheran) Synod of Ohio, began his ministry on the West Coast. He got to the lumber camps only once every three months. A couple of the congregations wanted the sacrament every Sunday, so old Mike Royce administered it. He was a lumberjack. On the frontier we were theologically very direct about some things; and then later we invented all kinds of ways to excuse what would actually be appropriate.

I come to the topic of ministry of the laity out of a genetically sound background. My father, a minister, had dignity; but my mother had the imagination in the family. I remember that she squirmed under the class structure in that old synod: there the laity were clearly the ground troops, and the clergy were the generals.

In the town where I grew up, my mother had great troubles with this. I remember that the district president, a particularly pompous man, came to preach at a conference. It was my turn to babysit (we had a large family) so my mother could go to church. When she returned I asked, "What did he say?"

She replied, "Nothing—for 30 minutes."

I also recall that when my older brother became a physician and began to practice in Chicago, he invited mother to come and visit him. He thought he would shock this woman from a little town in Ohio by taking her to a big city show. So they went to the famous road show, the Ziegfeld Follies. On the stage was a great 12-foot frame like a book, and as the door opened, the scantily clad ladies came out one by one—to the apparent delight of the audience. My brother thought that my mother would be taken aback by all this. But she was completely unflappable, taking it in stride, and said, "Thank you very much. I enjoyed the show."

Then next spring when the children of the parish school in father's congregation had a program, mother had the local carpenter build a big book, and out of the open book proceeded the little girls, each dressed like one of the women of the Bible. Now with the benefit of this imagination that could go from the Ziegfeld Follies to the Old Testament without batting an eyelash, I had a good early introduction to the ministry of the laity.

What does it mean that not only in the Lutheran church in the United States, but in various other bodies including the Roman Catholic Church, Christians are reinvestigating, reassessing, the meaning of the laity? What is the meaning of the rousing new life that is back of this topic emerging everywhere and with great energy?

First, we must consider the general world liberation movement that includes minority people as well as women. There is something happening in the 20th century that is, as it were, the broad theater within which the phenomenon we're talking about is but one theological or ecclesiastical aspect.

A sociologist friend of mine was musing about this one night when we were having dinner. He said, "I think the deepest meaning of the 20th century is that the baseline of the human is being enormously broadened." Think of humanity as a pyramidal structure. The baseline at the bottom of the pyramid is reaching upward. People in any culture we know about have always been ordered with very few at the top and then a layer down a few more, and so on. The baseline of billions had very little to do with what was going on at the top.

But what has happened in the 20th century is that the baseline of the human is swelling economically, politically, demographically, religiously, intellectually. We tend to look at this general liberation as being an indubitable good, and there is a sense in which I think this is true.

But the clear justice of a more general participation in the events and decisions that constitute our lives does not automatically deliver at the top. Twenty million Iranians may be just as wrong as one ayatollah. The American voting population may regard issues with such banality as to end up in the same situation as if one person, a banal leader, made all the decisions. Liberation, as such, does not automatically mean that everyone will be wiser, more prudent, more responsible. It simply means that our stupidity, as well as our prudence, will be distributed among more people.

All of this is relevant to the ministry of the laity; for that theater is not simply an ecclesiastical box or a theological item, though it is that. But it is happening within a general context in which more and more people are joining this ever-striving baseline of human participation in running their own lives.

I think this means that for the foreseeable political future, another 100 years at least, we're going to have troubled times in the world. You cannot convulsively tear down and then slowly recreate more and more humane forms of human existence. You cannot do that without passing through a time of troubles. But what our late unlamented vice-president, Spiro Agnew, with great unconscious irony, used to call "the decay of our moral fiber" may be the confusion that accompanies all great creative moments in history.

In any case, the theater of our reflections must be broadened beyond simply ecclesiastical concern. My own background in this context is, of course, Lutheran. We Lutherans are not absolutely peculiar human beings, though sometimes some of us act that way. But there is something peculiarly to be perceived and specified about looking at the ministry of the laity from a Lutheran focus.

The Lutheran perspective can contribute to avoiding two pathetic blunders that are characterizing the discussion of the issue in many parts of Christendom. First is that the word *ministry* is an absolutely unqualifiable term. That is, if we say every baptized person is a minister in Christ's church, we are right. But if we become uncritically indiscriminating about that asseveration, we may refuse to recognize forms of ministry within the generalized gift; our demands of ministry will then be unrealistic. There are church bodies in which the word *ministry* is being used in such a way, with such breadth and enthusiasm, that it is almost impossible, without seeming gauche or unspiritual, to introduce any reflective efforts of definition to the various forms of ministry.

Certainly it is imperative to stress the ministry of the laity. As Gustaf Aulen points out in *The Faith of the Christian Church*, from about A.D. 900 to 1200, a legalistic and wooden theory of atonement was being taught in the schools and written in the theological texts. But all the time this thing was being elaborated from the formation of the church, the good people out in front were still singing the vital doctrine of the atonement that is characteristic of the Gospel of Mark: that a strong man enters the prison in which pathetic human life is held by the demons and cracks open the door and brings them out. Aulen notes, "The bishops and the theologians were saying one thing from the front of the church, and the good old laity were singing, 'Christ lag in Todesbanden.' " All of us in our churches rejoice in the fact that the laity are being admitted to all levels of discussion and are invited to all levels of participation in the life of the church. But sometimes we do that on a "professional basis." That is, the lawyers, the business people, the analytical people, the sociologists, the economists, the eggheads among the laity are being brought into the discussion of the church because we need their expertise. Then we rejoice in the liberation of the laity. But we are very selective about which laity we admit—and this is wrong.

\*

Selfhood is not simply finding out and clarifying all the potentialities of the self as individual. There is no selfhood that is not at the same time a self existing in the grid of all selves. I have no self by myself—or for myself. I really have no identity that I can specify except the intersection point of a multitude of things that are not mine. They have been given to me. They are vitalities in history, in human life, and these all intersect at a point which is myself. And yet I know that that self is so richly intersected by others, not only those whom I meet personally but those whom I meet vicariously in the worlds of history and literature, that my self is only a point at which I acknowledge my own presence in the midst of so many things that are transindividual—more than myself.

Such a notion of identity is always in danger of a fateful reduction. I think of the notion of selfhood when I hear my students in their senior year talk about where they would like to exercise their ministry, and I hear them say that what they want most of all is self-fulfillment. There's something rather ghastly about that. I am not ordained to fulfill my precious self. One student had a list of things her first call had to have: it had to be in an urban setting; it had to be with certain kinds of Chicanos, blacks, and poor whites; it had to be in a cultural setting where she could enjoy theater and other activities. I said, "You know, it's as if the Bible says, 'Listen, Lord, thy servant speaketh,' instead of, 'Speak Lord, thy servant heareth.' The church is going to dump you someplace that may have little to do with your agenda. And it will offer the kind of challenge, humiliation, embarrassment, and opportunity that you didn't foresee." Our obedience in ministry cannot be calibrated with an agenda of clamant desires.

✳

I think how in my own life my preaching has changed in the some 55 years I have been at it. Now when I preach, I no longer proclaim: "This is the Word of God and you'd better believe it. The church teaches it; therefore, get with it." In the first place, that tennis ball bounces right back at you. The Word of God has a thundering authority of its own. It must reveal its own reality; it must testify of itself. I cannot hold people to believe on my authority, or the authority of the church. I've got to preach in such a way that the messages of the text—the energies of the reality of God—are disclosed in episode, parable, miracle story, and so on. They've got to do their work by their own intrinsic force, by the truth that they reveal.

## CHAPTER FIVE

# Theology: An Accumulation and a Doing

I would suggest that Christian theology is an act of faith whereby we invest a theory of episodes, symbols, metaphors, and historical reality with the most comprehensive meaning and truth we can imagine.

The *truth* of the Christian faith is not severable from the *meaning* of the Christian faith. It is the meaningfulness of a story composed of both the horrors and the delights of human existence. That is fundamentally what the faithful, the church, will depend on for the acceptance of its message. People will be attracted to or repelled by, find interesting or find dull, find relevant or find unintelligible, what we say and teach in exact relationship to its interpretive power.

That is the way Christian theology, in the long haul, has got to understand itself and defend itself. Jesus said that if you will obey and do the deeds, you will know the Spirit of truth (John 14:15-17). That means that the meaning appears only when the risk is taken; one cannot judge it from the outside.

✱

Theology is not just a church discipline or a discipline that is exercised by people who are religious. Socrates, Aristotle, Plato, Anaximander were all theologians. Before there were any Christians, there were theologians—people who wondered, to put it in Anaximander's terms, "What is that thing which is before everything, from which everything comes, and to which everything proceeds?"

Christian theology has several branches. First there is "biblical theology," the effort to make a systematic and coherent account of what the Scriptures say about God. It confines itself to the events, history, and statements that are made in the Scriptures, from Genesis to Revelation. Looking at that body of recorded data, human experience, reflection, pathos, and passion, it tries to systematize into understandable concepts what it says about the one who is beyond all others, that ground of all being which is under all that is. Biblical theology is usually subdivided into Old Testament theology and New Testament theology.

Then there are "historical theology"—the effort to record how theology developed from the earliest books of the Bible—and "confessional theology"—which operates primarily within the confessional theological statements of a particular community. Confessional theologians may be interested in theology in general, natural theology, philosophical theology, the theology of the Methodists, the Presbyterians, the Holy Rollers, and so on, but they are primarily concerned with the theology of their own confession.

The kind of theology I do shares with those three other fields. But my coming to maturity as a theologian took place only when I was transferred from the relatively amenable and friendly atmosphere of a church seminary into the slam-bang of a university faculty, where everybody's main response to a statement is, "How come? How do you know it? Why do you say that?" Theology, as I have been called in the last half of my life to practice it, has been carried on as a public activity, having to make its way on the stage of public criticism and public knowledge, amidst disciplines like physics, chemistry, mathematics, sociology, anthropology, and linguistics— and that is a difficult place to be a theologian.

My job at the University of Chicago was called *constructive theology*. My responsibility required that I, as both an individual and a representative of the community of faith, put that tradition on the battle line where theological affirmations meet general human affirmations: to reason and construct forward into a new situation the old statements of the church and the believing community.

For instance, I can say for myself and within my own community, "I believe in God, the Father almighty, creator of heaven and earth. I believe in Jesus Christ, his only Son, our Lord," and people nod their heads in a corporeal and corporate affirmation. They too affirm that. But in the university, the moment I say, "I believe in God," somebody says, "Why? By what right? By what reasonable ground do you dare say a thing like that?" So I have to take the whole tradition of accumulated Christian thought and put it forward as a public event in the face of those who don't believe it or who don't know whether they believe it. Theologians or preachers cannot make people believe. They can only explicate what it might mean to believe, in such a way as to lead others to entertain the possibility of believing.

I can offer an illustration. I was teaching in a typical

class made up of all sorts of men and women, some of them believers and some nonbelievers. (Not everyone who comes to a theological school in a university is headed for ordination; most of them are going to be teachers.) I was lecturing on the magnificent statement in the Nicene Creed about the relationship of Jesus the Son to the Father. A student sat there watching me with gimlet eyes. When I came near the conclusion, he raised his hand.

I said, "OK, what is it?"

He said, "You know, if it were true, it would do."

Now that is as far as a teacher can go. I can't transmit my sense of the truth of that statement to him, like writing out a prescription and letting him follow it. I can only teach in such a way as to engender in him the questions, as if he were saying to himself, "If it were true, it's a big enough truth that it would pull me together." In a sense, that's what a sermon is for: to hang the holy possible in front of the mind of the listeners and lead them to that wonderful moment when they say, "If it were true, it would do." To pass from that to belief is the work of the Holy Spirit, not of the preacher or the teacher.

A constructive theologian has a second job. He or she is supposed not simply to teach, transmit, and elaborate, but also to ask what meaning such a statement would have in view of the contemporary situation. That is to say, theology is not an accumulation only; it is a work. It is not just what people have thought, but it also investigates how the church's message might make sense, how its truth might be made clear, given the body of new learning in our generation.

For example, think of what enormous changes have taken place in the past 30 years in the study of cosmology. We now know, as we did not know so clearly when I was a boy, something about the enormous distances of the universe. We know a great deal that we did not know in the beginning of the 20th century about the various forms and activities of energy. We know a lot about the history of the cosmos. All of this must be admitted to the theater of theological reflection.

At the school with which I am now connected, they call me O. B.—Old Brooder. My main task is to sit and think. I am aided in that effort by the fact that my vision is now so bad that I cannot read. And while I lament that fact, I am also happy in certain fringe benefits (in fact, they're not fringe, they're central). When one cannot enjoy the constant input that reading affords, but must, as I do now, depend on readers and tapes, one has to think more about less. And I've found that in recent years I have probed more deeply into and reformulated for myself much in the church's theological tradition.

By *theology* I mean a reflection over and over and over again on the elemental events of the Christian community: the entire history of Israel that stands back of the events informing the new Israel. Those events, as they have been recalled and celebrated repeatedly throughout history, are like a certain amount of money put in a savings account. They accumulate an increment through the centuries. This accumulation is not like that of a tapeworm, sending out segment after segment of its own energy. The accumulation of theological terms, ideas, images happens because the remembered events are always encountering new situations in the human family, in the social world through history. They are not only pushed toward ever greater richness; they are drawn by events into ever fresh reflection.

When we talk of *theology*, we mean not only an accumulated mass of devotion, piety, reflection, intellectual work, historical documents. By *theology* we mean not only a having but a doing—not only an accumulated tradition, but a present task which must be done on the playing field of each generation in actual life. One *has* a theology, to a greater or lesser extent, in order to *do* theology, in order to exercise, administer, manifest this always forward movement.

I want to do theology in such a fashion that the mind may be invited to ask what is the relationship between the church and what I affirm about God and Christ. How does that illuminate some circumstance in culture? I do theology that way not simply because I chose to—although had I been utterly free of circumstances, I think I would have chosen it that way—but I do it quite frankly by accident. All my teaching career and my 13 years in the pastorate were lived on the margin of the church's life, where the church meets the world. My pastorate, during the very heart of the Depression, was in a little, beat-up, segmented congregation. I was ordained the week the stock market crashed; 70 percent of my people eventually were out of work in the midst of a great industrial city.

In my church we had no nursery, no crying room, no couple's club; we didn't have anything but a room, a hymnal, a pulpit, and an altar. So my early experience was never insulated or encapsulated within the church. I had to do theology on the street, where intellectual and cultural events were always pouring in on me.

✱

The church is no longer standing astride Western culture celebrating theology, the queen of the sciences, in command of a powerful, commonly believed tradition. Most people today not only do not believe the Christian faith; they do not know what its claims are.

We live in what has been called a Kleenex culture: build it, use it, throw it away. The very changes in our architecture are parabolic of the changes in the culture. Our technological society has determined that buildings are no longer solidifications of a tradition; they are simply functional housing for an operation. That's true not only of church buildings but of everything else. The Sears Tower in Chicago is estimated to be built for about half a century. And then the thing will be knocked down, and they'll build something equally bad.

The fundamental affirmations of Christian theology do not, like the Sears Tower, have a 50-year life span. But the language of their transmission, the images and human realities that constitute their proclaimed substance, must find their vocabulary and manner always in relation to the changing world.

The term "theology for the laity" is a phrase that invites the mind to a wrong image. The phrase suggests that really important theology is done in relative seclusion by special persons who command appropriate skills and write theological texts. This material, so the image suggests, is rare, difficult, often abstract and unavailable to the ordinary believer. So we further erroneously suppose that this good stuff must be watered down, reduced to obvious banalities, and retailed on Sunday morning to the patient customers.

Such a notion is both untrue and unfair. The academic theologian, like a researcher in any recondite body of knowledge, has the lonely obligation to use special skills to recover, clarify, order, and fashion appropriate conceptions.

A "theology for the laity" does not dilute that substance, banalize or oversimplify those findings, or make an obvious cliché out of a profound parable or other statement of Jesus. Theology for the laity is an exercise in language and reference whereby real substance intersects ordinary experience. "The fodder must be put down where the sheep can nibble," said Luther. But it must be real fodder.

My theology is not one derived from nature; it is a theology of the incarnation applied to nature—which is quite different.

I think it is because I came into theological work via the parish that I have always tested the usefulness of my own theological statements by their transmissability in the sermon—whether I could make sense of this thing to the faces that sat there on Sunday morning looking up at me.

My theological career has been a not-wholly-successful effort to drag my students out of the church—out of the church!—into what is happening in the world. My general effort was to lead them to appreciate the reality of the natural, the historical, the cosmological world of the galaxies in order that their theological speech would be intersective of the world their listeners take for granted.

*

Christian theology says that a person's being, self-hood, sense of who he or she is, is constituted by relationships in such a way that if any one of them is damaged, the individual's being is damaged.

Think about the word *being*. We're all used to the word *existence*. I can talk about my own existence, and I can point to the particularity of my autobiographical record. There is such a thing as the particularity of my existence over against yours; each of us can say this of himself or herself: "I was born in a particular place; I grew up with specific parents, went to certain schools."

But when I talk to you of *being*, I can only talk to you out of my existence and fling words across to the strangeness of your existence, which is in many ways other than mine. But I can do that and be understood because we have something in common that transcends the particularity of our existence.

What do we have that makes it possible to talk to one another? This is what we mean by being, human being, the essence or core of likeness that permits language and intelligibility, even if we have no language in common. For example, if I'm walking down a street in Bangalore, and a fat and pompous character struts out of a bank and slips on a banana peel, the observing Indian will laugh as loudly as I do. This response arises out of the depths of our being. All of life traverses a banana peel, and we all know it, whether in India, or East Asia, or Iceland, or Chicago. Christian theology affirms our connectedness.

# CHAPTER SIX

# Education
# as Furniture
# and Propellant

I am interested in education particularly from the standpoint of the deep sadness I feel when seeing students in theological declamations from the very day they are ordained. They will never know as much theology as they do in their senior year of seminary. Ten years later their general culture has been localized; their reading has been vastly diminished; their effort to understand what is going on in principal fields of inquiry—New Testament, church history, theology—is in many cases nonexistent. In places where I have been asked to help in adult education, I have tested this observation by bluntly putting a question to the group: "How many of you have read a New Testament introduction since you left the seminary?" Fewer than 10 percent will raise a hand.

In the ministry we somehow have the feeling that the intellectual, historical, and literary part of our preparation is something that can be deposited in us, or stuffed into us, in a period of three or four years; and we presume to run a whole lifetime on the original tankful.

When suddenly I had the job dropped in my lap of teaching Christian ethics, I had never read an entire textbook on the topic, and I knew it was too late to start scrounging around through 10 or 12 such books.

So I thought of a way to make the whole process of ethical thinking concrete. I selected four or five pieces of contemporary literature having ethical problems as themes, and then dismissed the class to read. I remember I gave the students Conrad's *Lord Jim,* Hemingway's *The Old Man and the Sea,* a series of short stories by Chekhov, Ibsen's *The Master Builder,* and Arthur Miller's *Death of a Salesman.* The dramatic content of these works revolves around a moral core: a moral problem, a failure, an act of dishonor or betrayal, a vague sense of a meaningless life.

Having read the material, the students were ready to hear me talk about ethics and what canons of obedience are appropriate for the Christian message. I didn't have to spark interest in the ethical questions; that was done by the artists.

I would use the same approach for continuing education. That is, don't start off simply with lectures, but find some way to evoke the kind of question that requires a better answer than the students have received from their earlier education. For instance, why not send out reprints of a case study that concludes with an agonizing problem in medical ethics about whether to prolong life or let die. Ask, "At what point is the problem ethical, Christian? What has God got to do with the matter?" This is real education.

There are few things more futile than answering questions no one is asking. When I am called on to do two or three evenings with a group of people, whenever I know far enough ahead, I say to the inviter, "If you will have your people read a couple of things I will send you, then I will come." Otherwise, I come and am expected to be a kind of high-level entertainer. Well, I have enough debts, and my rent is steep enough that I would gladly take the money for it, but I don't feel good about it. The people are not sitting there open, precise, sharpened-up to hear someone address a pressing question.

People do not always respond as I might wish. For example, I was once asked by a group of pastors to discuss Reginald Fuller's *The Formation of the Resurrection Narratives* and responses to it. And I said, "I will not come unless you promise, every last one of you, to read Reginald Fuller" (this was months ahead of the event). The group inviting me had about 90 members, but only about 40 said they would read the book. (I went anyway.) However, the 40 who said they would do it—and did—spent a day in discussion and then wanted another. It was a real educational experience for them. I served in the capacity of ink; they were the blotter.

How can one's college years be spent in such a way that they are not a period of diminishment from religious understanding or a laming of true piety? Most students at our denominational schools have come from families in which, with greater or lesser intensity, the Christian tradition has been represented. In college a student presumably multiplies his or her person, joins the human race, moves away from a province into a great world. These are years of growth in which the individual progresses from a personally centered idea of the *self* into a notion of *selfhood* that is constituted by a vaster and profounder world than he or she knew as a child. The college years should indeed offer the opportunity for such opening outward.

Now, while this growth is taking place, the whole religious tradition comes under scrutiny; in fact, it often comes under such scrutiny as leads to its rejection. Often this happens because the student's religious tradition may not seem able to keep pace in its intellectual structure with what he or she is learning in college. During such a period, what a student's intellectual maturation demands is an expanding doctrine of God. The simpler doctrine of God that is rightly and necessarily the one we learn as children remains tightly enfolded within the language, within categories that are simply incapable of filling the space of one's growing intellectual experience.

However, neither lamentations nor castigation of the students is the right way to get at the problem. The way to do that is to ask the faculty to come together to talk about theological enrichment and growth in theological discourse. In fact, these teachers were probably victims of the same circumstances during their own college years.

I meet many faculty people who, despite the enormously sophisticated research they do, are living with an adolescent or childhood notion of God, which is seemingly unable to open any discourse with their learned discipline. Therefore they simply create a compartment. On Sunday they are devout, pious Christians. During the rest of the week they are physicists, chemists, biologists, or what not, and there is no intersection or crossover among the categories in which they live.

Fundamentally, one cannot live in this fragmented way. One may seem to bring it off. But the first result of these sealed compartments of discourse is that one's own area of specialty suffers. Second, the interior stress creates an intolerable personality tension (one which I have sensed in many of my university colleagues).

Thus the church-related college and its faculty must make conscious efforts to incorporate high-level theological study into the institution's general curriculum. For, indeed, the Christian faith is entirely capable of the ever more capacious interpretation that can parallel a student's or a teacher's expanding needs and understandings.

Wherever did we get the idea that only the "childish" is available or accessible to children? Where did we get the notion that only the absurdly reduced symbol is open to the child's imagination? We teach the children to sing "This is my Father's world," which is a good theological statement, but then we follow it up with little stories about the pansies and the kitty cats. Children can also know something beyond playthings.

Students eventually come to us at the seminary in such a riddled condition, with such an inadequate theology, because we have not thought the growing child's mind capable of including larger references to the meaning of the Word of God and the church.

Our humane education has shriveled under the pressure of our bureaucratic obligations. Our humanity itself becomes bureaucratized, routinized. This shrinkage of our educated and clerical humanity is one of the most discouraging aspects of my life. It is not that I expect the clergy to become theologians in the professional sense, though every ordained one should be a theologian. Nor do I expect them to be great scholars. But I do expect them to be alive human beings; and I do not find this aliveness in proper intensity among many of today's improperly educated clergy.

When I refer to intellectual content, I do not mean big words. For example, consider St. Augustine's sentence, "Thou has made us for thyself, O Lord; and our hearts are restless until they rest in thee." That is not incomprehensible to anyone. But how many preachers might reach or explore the depths of it with the common people? I preach to congregations of working people as much as I do to those at colleges and universities. And I preach the same sermons. I might use illustrative material that is more appropriate and intelligible and evocative here than there, but the content of the thought is the same. By intellectual I do not mean abstract, multisyllabic, cerebrally impenetrable. I mean reflective—articulating the way something is. That can actually be done very simply.

If you ask me what makes a good teacher, I can tell you that he or she gives off the notion, "What I'm talking about is enormously important and alluring and exciting, and I wish you knew more about it." When that happens in a classroom, there is something worthwhile going on.

I remember a great, great teacher I once knew. He was a little, wispy, absentminded fellow who taught Romantic and Victorian poetry. The rest of the faculty regarded him as somewhat odd, and he was. He was so wrapped up in 19th-century pastoral poetry that he didn't pay much attention to grades. Therefore all the football players took his courses.

One day I sat in on one of his classes. At the end of the period, the professor said, in his soft voice, "Next Friday, gentlemen, you will have read when you come to my class, 'The Intimations of Immortality' by Wordsworth. I wish you to come with your minds gloriously adorned." The funny thing was that those hulking, generally not-too-bright football players made the effort. For the man took the students more seriously than they took themselves. He didn't see why a fellow who was a tackle on Saturday shouldn't love Wordsworth. He invested his students with his confidence and the possibility that Wordsworth is every person's possession. This is teaching at its best.

College faculty should be educated persons. This is often not the case. Many of them are trained—not educated. You can train dogs to jump, and you can train people to report what is going on in chemistry and transmit that information. But education means training the mind to unfold to the multiple facets of human existence with some appreciation, eagerness, and joy. It is, in essence, the opposite of being dull. We've got plenty of trained, dull people on our faculties, but not many educated people.

CHAPTER SEVEN

# Language:
# Allure and Boundary

In the process of being idiomatic, new Bible translations have subtly but importantly modified many dimensions of the older versions. Remember the beautiful observation, "Consider the lilies of the field, how they grow; they toil not, neither do they spin" (Matt. 6:28 KJV). We don't talk much about "toil" any longer; instead we go to work. One modern translation reads: "Look at those lilies." That is a quite different statement. With the former construction, the language lies tenderly upon the thing referred to. Love, affection, and tenderness are inherent in the language.

Then, too, the word *consider* has an intrinsic warmth that the word *look* cannot manage.

That's the *spirit* of the mind, not just the *work* of the mind. The work of the mind can make up all kinds of sentences, but the spirit of the mind has a feeling for what language is appropriate to a particular situation.

*

Our generation has lost its ear for multidimensional language. Yet without some recovery of that language, I think we are going to have a very difficult time transmitting the Scriptures to future ages. In modern translations of the Bible we have gained exactitude at the price of loveliness; we have won precision at the cost of internal rhetorical beauty.

In the parish of which my father was pastor the Christmas Eve service read, "And when the days were accomplished that she should be delivered. . . ." The pastor for a recent radio vespers on Christmas Eve did a paraphrase of the ancient narrative. He said, "Now when the time came for Mary to have a baby. . . ."

That is simply not the same statement. Biologically it points to the same event, but religiously it is not the same. What is the difference? I love the old rendering because it says that what is happening in the event is something that God is bringing about; it has a quasi-mystical ring to it. Further, it emphasizes a period of waiting, and that is an important part of the story.

Or take another example. In the Magnificat, is it the same statement when we say, "My soul magnifies the Lord" as when we say "My soul doth magnify the Lord"? There is a difference between the two. "My soul doth magnify the Lord" is rich in intentionality, bespeaking a focused will. The former is simply a statement of fact.

One final example: What is the difference between addressing God as *you* or as *thou*? We somehow feel that we haven't lost anything by that change, but I don't agree. We have lost something when we use the same kind of language for God that we use with one another.

It is fundamental to our understanding of God that he is not one of us. He became one of us, but in himself he is God and not a human.

The awesome, mystical, stunning difference between God and the creatures is an important difference. Why have we found it necessary to use informal language about God when, on the other hand, we sing "O Canada, we stand on guard for thee" or "My country 'tis of thee"? Whenever we want to raise a thing to a certain level, formal speech is an outward and visible sign of that elevation. When we lower it, we lose something meaningful.                    ✱

I don't know when it was that I first had my attention called to the combination of precision and magic that words contain. As I reflect back, I still remember how, as a child of about seven or eight, when I couldn't really understand all of the exalted language, I nevertheless listened week after week to my father as, in a beautiful voice, he read the order of worship. And I remember how certain phrases stuck in my mind. I didn't know exactly what father meant when, reading the liturgy at the Communion, he said, "And therefore with angels and archangels and all the company of heaven," but I knew it was something very big.

And I've never forgotten the beautiful prayer that was appointed for All Saints' Day in the common service book before we reduced our language to absolute flat-footedness. "O Almighty God, Who hast knit together Thine elect in one communion and fellowship in the mystical Body of Thy Son. . . ." Somehow today, apparently, we think that's too fancy; but the figure is magnificent. Paul talks about the body of Christ. But the prayer, in a perfectly gorgeous image, talks about the body of Christ and each one of us in it. If you've watched someone knit, you've seen how each stitch is interlocked with every other stitch in such an integral way that if one stitch is dropped, the whole line ravels apart. That's exactly what Paul meant when he said that if one of us suffers, the whole body suffers. But how beautifully the prayer catches it up: "Who hast knit together thine elect . . . in the mystical body of thy Son."

The most accelerated way into understanding what Scripture or any other piece of great literature means is by a fastidious attention to the language. Such fastidiousness is hard to come by these days. We are so benumbed and slugged and diverted, day and night, by radio and television, and in the process we hear language so demeaned and so exaggeratedly used, that the very ability to use words with clarity, precision, and lucidity has become a rare practice in our time.

H e that hath seen me hath seen the Father." How could Jesus say those words and mean them literally? He didn't. We don't see God, ever. God is not a datum or a phenomenon. When Jesus said, "He who hath seen me hath seen the Father," his language did not refer to a visual record on some retina. That would be blasphemous to both Jew and Christian. We shall see God face to face, and I know the meaning of that language. And I hope for it to happen. But I don't intend some day to look at some heroic-sized man like unto myself and say, "This is God."

W hen shall we dwell in the presence of God? In the book of Revelation, the last appearance is described: "Who are these, clothed in white robes, and whence have they come? . . . God will wipe away every tear from their eyes" (Rev. 7:13, 17). This is the picture of the new Jerusalem.

What kind of language is that? It is symbolic, eschatological, even apocalyptic language. It's a marvelous way of saying, "Eye has not seen, nor ear heard." How could it? All that my eye has seen has got to be that which my eye, being temporal, mortal, earthly, can see. But beyond what I can see is that which, as God gives the promise, shall be given. No language can truly describe that.

\*

Of the great Christian or Jewish words—God, love, sin, guilt, forgiveness, reconciliation—none is a definition. They are all relational statements. That is, love is not a thing; it is a relation. Guilt is not a thing; it is a relation. Sin, too, is not a thing; it is a relation. In reconciliation, the prefix re- means conciliation reestablished, or harmony once broken put back together. This is terribly important. When I say you cannot find a definition of love, I mean that love becomes clear and recognizable only when you behold a relationship.

For example, sin is a broken relationship. The very first chapter of Genesis reveals that *adam* (which is not a proper name, but a Hebrew word for humankind) and *eve* (the mother of all the living) represent the whole human family as before the one who called them into existence. And what's the first thing they do? Call into question God's lordship. They say, "We, too, want to know something about all of this; we want control, we want to have knowledge." That is the heart of sin: human beings alienate themselves, separate themselves, cut themselves off from God.

There is a kind of speech that I would call evocative speech. It uses language that does not have the mathematical precision of designative speech but that has the strange power to cause us to remember—to cast our minds back to visions that we have shared with the speaker—to cause us in our imagination to come alive and with a kind of pathos join ourselves to that object to which the speech addresses itself. Let me give you an illustration.

In Shakespeare's *Romeo and Juliet*, Romeo must by decree leave Juliet at dawn. Shakespeare speaks of the rising sun as the "jocund sun." There is a bitter and evocative joke delivered by that adjective. Romeo calls the sun "jocund" because the sun knows nothing of the anguish of the two lovers. And the term evokes a common experience. How much of the great world unknowingly passes by the solitary despair?

*

In my own passage from an ordinary, as it were, pagan childhood (any adolescent boy who is not part pagan is not fully boy), one factor was the stories of the New Testament, the stories of the words and deeds and teachings of Jesus.

Indeed, I have to say that my whole life has been haunted by the reality of Jesus. What do I mean by *haunted*? First, there is the Gospels' record concerning Jesus. Take one aspect of that reality. The New Testament community greeted Jesus with all kinds of words, ascriptions, and titles; but what fascinated me when I first learned of it—and it has not ceased to fascinate me to this day—is the way in which Jesus both wore and rejected the titles. The community used the language of the hope of Israel to acknowledge the presence of this phenomenon, Jesus of Nazareth, and they flung over him the rhetorical garments of their expectation: he is the king, he is the Messiah, he is the son of David, he is the Son of man, the Son of God, the anointed one, he that should come. This was the whole rich language of Israel's expectation of God's most mighty act. This language was wrapped round Jesus.

The interesting thing is that Jesus does not appear to have rejected it, nor did he explicitly adopt it. He seems always to have acknowledged what the intention was of those who used that kind of language for him, but he was never content to shrink the dimensions of his reality to the language of our expectations. This fascinates me. We use the language of our expectation as a descriptive, ascriptive, Christological statement.

Jesus himself lives within that language, but he always slips out and exceeds its nature and intentionality. There is a certain moment, for instance, when one of the Gospels reports that a woman stood before him admiring, thrilled by the words from his lips and muttering (perhaps only to herself, but he heard it), "How happy is the woman who bore you and nursed you!" And with great abruptness, almost brusqueness, Jesus said, "Rather, how happy are those who hear the word of God and obey it!" (Luke 11:27-28 TEV). In every situation in which an effort was made to say, "Aha! Now we know who you are. Now we have the linguistic label whereby to pin down the secret of your reality," Jesus seems quietly or openly to slip away from the confines of our own ascription and to affirm a beyondness. That objective fact is an element in my reference to "the haunting figure of Jesus."

I say so much about language, and with such passion, because of my certainty that matter and manner are inseparable, that substance and form cannot be split, that the what and the how are irrevocably linked.

Scriptural speech about God is always dynamic. God is what God does. God is that from which all things come. This means that God language is fundamentally functional—not propositional. It has the dynamism of something always alive and becoming. Perhaps it has something to do with my having had a double major—religion and biology—in college, but I have never understood God as some ecstatic value mold spewing out creative energies.

Sometimes we have taken the admonition in the Epistles of St. John, "Do not love the world" (1 John 2:15), to mean that we ought as Christian and pious people to walk through the world holding our noses, as it were, as if God's creation somehow smelled bad and we ought not get too close to it. However, the verse certainly cannot have that meaning, because God made the whole world, and meant it—all of it—to be loved.

I have been reflecting on when and where I first learned to carry on a lover's relationship with the physical world. I think it began in elementary school, when I had a remarkable teacher whose name was Miss Davis, as I now recall it with affection. She had a habit which would be regarded in these days with disdain by educational theorists. She began each class session with a bit of writing of memorable beauty, and some of those

things she read to us runny-nosed, cap-askewed little
kids haunt me to this day. I think my love affair with
the natural world began on hearing the lines she read
to us.

We sometimes suppose that people look upon the
world and find it beautiful and then look for a language
with which to adorn what they behold. I think that is
true, but it also works the other way. Sometimes we are
partly blinded toward this world, and then someone
puts the beauty of which we had not been aware into a
gorgeous line. Thereafter we behold it in a new way. We
go not only from beholding to language, but we may go
from the beauty of language to the enhancement of beholding.

One of the selections Miss Davis read to us was from
the last act of *The Merchant of Venice* when the great action
has really finished and the young lovers are united. Lor-
enzo leads Jessica out into the night, and then come the
beautiful lines:

> *How sweet the moonlight sleeps upon this bank!*
> *Here will we sit, and let the sounds of music*
> *Creep in our ears: soft stillness and the night*
> *Become the touches of sweet harmony.*
> *Sit, Jessica. Look, how the floor of heaven*
> *Is thick inlaid with patines of bright gold:*
> *There's not the smallest orb which thou behold'st*
> *But in his motion like an angel sings,*
> *Still quiring to the young-eyed cherubins (V.i.55-63).*

I learned to look at the sky in a different way by virtue
of hearing that passage.

And then as a lad growing up in the small Ohio town
where my father was a pastor, I learned further to look
at the world in a kind of fascinated and determined way.

I owed part of this further fascination to the first four lines of John Keats' "The Eve of St. Agnes":

> *St. Agnes' Eve—Ah, bitter chill it was!*
> *The owl, for all his feathers, was a-cold;*
> *The hare limped trembling through the frozen grass,*
> *And silent was the flock in woolly fold.*

Anyone who has lived in the country or in a small town will resonate to that passage. All of my life I've been a passionate lover of our rich American land's variety: the lonely beauty of New England, the great chain of the Appalachians and the Green and White Mountains, the sweep of the prairies, the majesty of the Rockies, the unbelievable fecundity of the West Coast valleys. It all comes to expression in lines by Walt Whitman which Miss Davis first read to me. It occurs in his "Song of the Exposition," in which the undulating length of the lines is so like the undulating shape of the land in Iowa and Nebraska:

> *Thy limitless crops, grass, wheat, sugar, oil, corn, rice,*
> *   hemp, hops,*
> *Thy barns all fill'd, the endless freight-train and the bulg-*
> *   ing storehouse,*
> *The grapes that ripen on thy vines, the apples in thy*
> *   orchards,*
> *Thy incalculable lumber, beef, pork, potatoes, thy coal,*
> *   thy gold and silver,*
> *The inexhaustible iron in thy mines.*

Is it not possible that we can learn to regard the world as a place of grace, because there have been those among our fellows who have celebrated it in such language that the transcendent grace of God resonates and is reflected in the common grace of the creation?

# CHAPTER EIGHT

# Modern Culture

It is estimated that between 55 and 60 million persons watch soap operas every day. I am not a soap opera buff, but anything that that many people do is intrinsically of interest to anyone who wants to talk to the culture. So once when I was stuck between appointments in San Antonio, Texas, I thought, *Now's the chance!*

I had a television in my room at the hotel, and from nine until three, with a corned beef sandwich at noon, I watched six soap operas, one right after the other, for two days. I began to watch, I admit, with a certain attitude of intellectual superiority. But after about two hours I began to get interested and to take note of a certain continuity in each of the dramas. The problems are the same; the issues are the same; the picture of human life in each of them is a different scenario, but nevertheless, with a wearisome regularity, pushes up the same kind of human problem. This picture of human life is partly true and partly phony.

The setting is particularly phony. There are never any dirty dishes in the sink in a soap opera. The woman never looks as if she were too busy to get herself into perfect shape. She's always beautiful, always well-dressed.

But the soap operas, for all of their phoniness, say something about our culture: especially that, despite all its busy communication and community organization, it is a very lonely one. Second, it's a culture that longs for elemental speech—speech that does not trip over the cosmetic surface of life with the usual comments ("Have a good day!"), but speech that pierces down and looks another person straight in the eye and asks, "What's the matter?" or "Where is it that you're hurt?"

The soap opera is magnificent in its reflection of the problematic of human existence, but it's phony, too, in the rapidity of its solution. The soap opera elaborates the human problematic or the contradiction, the ambiguity, loneliness, or value-sloppiness of human life very well. But what's bad is that it offers a very tiny prescription for a very sick situation. The problem person is so very often automatically taken out of the role by being hit by a truck. Or the nasty problem person goes off to Miami Beach and dies of something. The solutions are too snappy, too quick, too unrealistic. They are not concomitant with the size of the problem.

A necessary address by the Christian gospel to the problems that the soap opera dramatizes must probe deeply into the loneliness, guilt, betrayal, and grief that this kind of program consistently portrays.

\*

For seven years during my tenure at the University of Chicago I had a committee appointment at the medical school. Along with a legal expert I worked with a committee to monitor all experimentation involving human subjects (the committee is required by law to include two nonphysicians). No proposal asking for a grant to carry out research could be approved without the unanimous consent of this group. Just as someone once said war is too important to be left to the generals, so medical research is too important to be left to the physicians. So, for seven years I got a firsthand, often frightening, look at what is going on in medical research.

The Christian faith has always been called on to deliver guides for life, to suggest appropriate action in various moral circumstances. Christian ethics has become an enormous body of judgment, opinion, and directives for living. But I came to learn that there is simply nothing in Scripture that gives us much help as we look for a way to deal Christianly with some current medical problems.

Existence can now be sustained mechanically beyond the time when it has any characteristics of real human life. The human body can be made electronically to continue its vital signs when it no longer has the strength to emit them on its own. Is one dead or not when those signs are mechanically sustained?

Today's medical problems did not exist for earlier generations. When I was young, the flu epidemic of 1917 and 1918 killed an estimated nine million people in this country because there were no antibiotics. I remember that my father was busy day after day with funerals. Once he came home and said of a certain man who had been my Sunday school teacher, "Well, Mr. Miller died today of the old man's friend." We don't hear that phrase anymore, but in those days it meant pneumonia. When old people became very ill and were immobilized for a large part of the time, fluid gathered in the lungs, and they died of pneumonia. It was a friend in the sense that it brought them the relief of death and usually came painlessly.

Today Mr. Miller wouldn't get pneumonia, or, if he got it, he would be hit with the specific antibiotic that deals with pneumococcus. He would survive the old man's friend and die of a degenerative disease. And even if he reached the age of 85 and had heart failure, the heart can be kept going, and the kidneys be made to function, and so forth. So we have now a new situation for which the old ethical guides are simply no longer sufficiently illuminative.

This all adds up to a new theological task for our time: to probe for ways of making morally responsible decisions in the midst of novel moral situations. Birth control, the problem of abortion, the care of severely retarded children, the definition of death, the pros and cons of life-sustaining facilities require this new theological project.

In terms of scriptural guidance, we are called on in many situations today to substitute responsible judgment for clear direction. We have no clear law to follow. We must make a judgment in the midst of an indeterminate situation without the serenity of knowing we have made the right or the Christian one. That is the problem of the contemporary pastor, teacher, relative, or friend.

Do we have any Christian symbol that might help us in such a situation? I find one in the offertory of the church. As any teenager will tell you, the offertory is the collection; but that is not its original meaning. The offertory is that turning point in the service when adoration, ascription, celebration, the declaration of the Word of God in the office of the Word have been completed, and now the service turns, and the offering of response is made. That this may be made in terms of gifts is one meaning, but it is also calling on the people to offer themselves in response to God's grace.

In a sense, when one makes an ethical judgment in an indeterminate situation, that judgment might be seen as an offertory. "This seems to me the right and the most morally appropriate thing to do. I offer it to God in the hope that it may be acceptable, but if it is not, then I can simply rest, in my own ignorance, on the forgiveness of God."

The Eucharistic Prayer in the Lutheran *Service Book and Hymnal* includes an ancient phrase about our offertory response: "not as we ought, but as we are able." Is it not possible that this phrase may point to a way of acting devoutly but not absolutely, a way of offering a judgment without the conviction of its certain righteousness?

Cannot the church do any better than to house the gravity of its functions in the busy, nervous, ridiculous buildings that it so often selects? Chopped-up and noisy, church office buildings are frequently like the billing room for Continental Can Company.

By contrast, I think of the beautiful old building at the University of Chicago that houses the Divinity School. It is in the Gothic style: old-fashioned, grave, dignified, rocky. There is not a false piece of material in it. The floors are real slate, not plastic tiles. The windows are

real. The decor is quiet and serene. It is celebrative out-
wardly of what we are supposed to be about inwardly.

Too many church-related buildings look like they
could just as well house some insurance company. The
faculty in many seminaries sit in rows of little cubicles,
one indistinguishable from another. In that way we become indistinguishable from one another. I don't know
how we stumbled into the stupidity we have committed
whereby we affirm grace and create banality, affirm
beauty and create ugliness. It makes no sense at all.

In the uses of literature, the uses of art, I find our
intellectual obligation being unfulfilled. We simply are
not cultivated people in our time. Of the old church an
ancient historian said, "The church in the first three centuries won the empire because it outlived, it out-
thought, and it outdied the pagan world"—including in
intellectual and artistic achievement. But much of the
intellectual and aesthetic life within the contemporary
congregation is simply contemptible. The intellectual
content of the ordinary sermon is contemptible. It is
often full of moral fervor and piety, but it is usually
absent in the clarity of ideas that thread against the accepted norms and offer new possibilities for reflection.

How is it possible that our church social room should
be filled with pictures that are mostly *Kitsch*, to use that
eloquent German word, when centuries of artists have
taken religious symbols and given them eloquent
expression? I am continually amazed by the fact that
something happens when one becomes pious. Is the
price of piety stupidity? Is the result of being devout
that one becomes intellectually and aesthetically insen-
sitive so that the actualities of this world are no longer
available to us?

*

We must somehow become less frenetic in activity and more dedicated to reflection. Maybe we should write less and ponder more, travel less and reflect more, say fewer things but better things. I find so little of this in the church today.

I am not saying we must ignore science and technology. For example, some years ago an architect whom I had long known was invited to build a chapel for the Illinois Institute of Technology, where most of the architecture is in the Bauhaus style—very technological and mathematical. So my friend designed a beautiful chapel in that style. But when he designed a stainless-steel altar rail, all the people on the building committee became upset. They thought of course that altar rails are all made of wood and that they are all manufactured in Grand Rapids, Michigan. They were offended. "You can't use a bare metal like that as an altar rail," they complained.

But the formula for stainless steel was worked out at this institution, and stainless steel is a beautiful product. Why not shape stainless steel to the glory of God? This was my friend's view, and he was quite right. His attitude was a refinement of aesthetics: using a material so as to honor it, using it in its proper context.

Materials are important. There is a beautiful Lutheran church in Eugene, Oregon, designed by Pietro Belluschi. As one walks into that church, one becomes silent. It shuts you up, literally. There is something about the proportion, the use of materials, the combination of strength and serenity in that church that is utterly right.

It is not magic. Belluschi did things that are specifiable. He used a high brick wall in the back of the altar that doesn't look like just any brick wall. When one gets close to it, one sees that those bricks are laid in and out so that they cast tiny shadows and give a depth of texture to the wall. One wonders why sounds reverberate so magnificently and finds out that the architect did careful planning, making use of the mathematical laws of acoustics. It is possible to reduce serenity to mathematics. We can accomplish these moods not by prayer alone, though the architect may have prayed about it. It is possible to use management of known principles in the creation of a church without rendering it banal or ugly.

We ought not permit the meaning of the term *experience* to be confined within the brackets of one's own existence. The meaning of experience is a poor and haggard thing if it refers only to what has happened to me. The meaning of education and of culture is that we live vicariously a thousand other lives, and all that has happened to human beings, things that have been recorded not by my experience but by the experience of others, become a second life, and a third, and so on. I'm annoyed by those who define experience by saying, "Well, I haven't met it yet; it hasn't happened to me. Therefore, it has no authority." I would be a poor person if the only things I knew were what I have found out for myself.

Through great poetry and drama and essays I have experienced things that my own bracketed life never permitted me to experience firsthand. I have sailed the seas with Captain Ahab in *Moby Dick*. I have lived in a

hundred strange places with Ernest Hemingway and
Nathaniel Hawthorne. By reading Joseph Conrad, a particular favorite of mine, I have learned something of the
horror of estrangement, alienation, and the life-destroy-
ing energies of loneliness.

I have known how to comprehend my own moral
embarrassment by the magnificent achievement of
Shakespeare's *Hamlet*. In *Othello* and *Macbeth* I have
known something of human terror—to which the fairly
pleasant and confined limits of my life gave me no access. Hamlet and King Claudius and Gertrude are more
real than real, because they are the compressed essence
of every king, and every queen, and every titled person
before a moral problem. They are the fine essence of
human reality. They are truth.

At one moment in the liturgy we cry, "Kyrie eleison,"
"Lord, have mercy." One contemporary musical
setting for that phrase much annoys me, and I have
reflected on why that is. Then I realized that the phrase
is a supplication; the musical setting sounded like a demand!

Traditional musical settings had a variety of forms,
but they were all characterized by gravity. I am not sure
you can be grave with the time beat this generation likes.
I remember an old Sam Johnson statement that the jollity
of the clergy much displeased him. Well, much contemporary liturgy is just too jolly! In the Christian faith there
is certainly a mood of celebration and thanksgiving. But
when one gets beyond the age of 25 or so, the celebrative
mood is no longer adequate to one's deepening awareness of life's ambiguities. The God of our worship is

indeed Lord of the dance; but there are nondanceable requirements that he is obliged to satisfy. So this jollification of the liturgy, this bounciness of the musical lines, is an appropriate mode for some occasions; it is bitterly inappropriate for others.

I am not here appealing for mordancy. Nor do I believe that the Gregorian chant is the necessary model for all liturgical music, but I am violently protesting against its disappearance. The old stance of the church that floats with a timeless, high impersonality—this is the very essence of the Christian God-relationship. This was before I was; this will be when I am gone. God's initiative toward me does not hang on the vagaries of my subjectivity. There is something in the old chants of the church that brought a necessary, audible balance to the self-incurvature of contemporary Christianity, and I very much lament its loss.

God is interested in a lot of things besides religion. God is the Lord and Creator of all life, and there are manifestations of the holy in its celebration or in its repudiation—in every aspect of the common life. The stories of Flannery O'Connor, for instance, are not theological treatises, but they unfold the pathos and the delight of the human condition. The novels of Saul Bellow are a wonderful exposition of people who stand within a powerful, though half-forgotten, religious tradition, and who are forced by the exigencies and tragedies of life back to the deep fountains that they have long covered over.

The problem of God—whether or not God is and what is his disposition toward human creatures, and what

God's intent is in nature, history, and human life—pops up under a million labels, all the way from Wallace Stevens to Joyce Carol Oates. The problem of God eludes human labels, but God clearly does not fall simply within the confines of religious discussion.

The women of my acquaintance who are interested in the liberation of their sex seem to be utterly unfamiliar with four important female writers: Jane Austen, the Brontë sisters, and George Eliot. Jane Austen, for example, was a moralist who touched the nature of good and evil, not with a sledgehammer but with a delicate, probing knitting needle. Of the Brontë sisters, Charlotte, in her battle for recognition in a male-dominated business, made with passionate strength every salient point that then took 100 more years to resurface.

The force of the feminist movement would be greatly strengthened if its contemporary vehemence was more deeply rooted in the larger and older chorus that cried out against earlier injustice.

The first time I saw a digital watch, I was annoyed, and it didn't take much reflection on my part to arrive at the reason. Time is a mysterious thing; we all lie drenched in its passingness. The watch that has a hand moving slowly around and marking the minutes of the hours and the hours of the day is a physical representation of the nature of time. But a watch that jumps from one second to another is a misrepresentation of the continuity. "Time like an ever-rolling stream," the old hymn says. The ever-rolling stream has flow and continuity. A watch calls my attention to or celebrates that character of time; a digital watch is a misrepresentation of the deep and primitive wonder before the mystery of time.

The malleability of all things, the pathos of time's passingness, the forward-looking, irrecoverable nature of time—this is a theme central to the human reality. The gospel speaks from within and to mortality and passingness, and for that reason a sense of time as both irrecoverable and promising characterizes the deepest wisdom. The nervous, jerky, digital watch would, I think, have been offensive to the writer of Psalm 90: "So teach us to number our days that we may get a heart of wisdom."

\*

There is today a general religious bias toward a galloping subjectivity. But our first obligation to a text is to let it hang there in celestial objectivity—not to ask what it means *to us*. A good sermon or a good teaching job must begin with angelic objectivity.

There's something in the mood of our culture that hates that. We want to hurry up and get to what something means to the individual. But this notion presents a serious danger for the true meaning of any important text—biblical, literary, or otherwise. The text had a particular meaning before I saw it, and it will continue to mean that after I have seen it. It expresses an intention that is meant to be heard by all, not interpreted according to any one individual's preferences or biases.

\*

My son, then a teenager, and I were watching the first moon shot together. I was all worked up about this really uncanny event back then in the 1960s. Knowing as I did something about cosmology, I was simply stunned by the magnificence of this accomplishment—landing a man on the moon! My kid sat there; he didn't even take his feet off the table. He noticed that I had my jaw hanging out, and he said, "Don't worry, Pop, they'll make it."

That response was almost parabolic. He took for granted a world that I have striven for a long time to understand at all. Your children, and your children's children, are already growing up in a world in which the doctrine of God has got to swing in the same orbits with the sun, the moon, and the farthest stars. A generation that learns about modern physics in the fifth grade and lives with complete aplomb in an electronic world is not likely to find its Sunday school picture of God adequate to its everyday experience.

CHAPTER NINE

# The Necessity
# and Embarrassment
# of Choice

The Holocaust of the 1940s was an event that left all
intellectual and moral reflection in a state of shock.
The disclosures that were occasioned by those events
have meant that no intellectual reflection can ever be the
same, and no moral statement about the nature of humanity can ever again be as unreflective as was formerly
possible.

It has been possible in some ages of Western history
to keep the problem of evil a neutral, indeterminate one,
and in long periods it has evoked very little common
interest. But the event of the Holocaust has brought the
problem of evil thunderingly to the center of every intelligent person's mind and spirit.

By the problem of evil, I mean something very simple,
though the simplicity of the statement has nothing to
do with the complexity of the problem. If God is good,
if God created and is the Lord of his creation, why does

evil exist? Why in a creation of a good God do the de-
monic powers of evil seem not only to exist but to grow
and wreak appalling human suffering?

Let me begin by saying that there is a phrase in Scripture which I think must be cast over the reflections that
follow. The phrase is "the mystery of God." There is
always a disposition in religious experience and in intellectual, theological reflection to assume that we can
penetrate more profoundly into that mystery than, in
fact, we are ever able to do. There is a great text in the
Old Testament on which I have never had the nerve to
preach: "I am the Lord, and there is no other. I form
light and create darkness, I make weal and create woe,
I am the Lord, who do all these things" (Isa. 45:6b-7).

Is there an answer to the problem of evil? I want to
make a distinction between seeking an answer to a problem and seeking a reply to a problem. I would suggest
at the outset that there never can be an answer to the
problem of evil. But in both Judaism and Christianity
there are replies to the problem of evil.

Imagine a little child awakening in the middle of the
night and the mother coming into the room to hear her
child say, "I'm scared."

The mother says, "There's nothing to be frightened
about. There's really no bear in the closet. There's nothing under your bed."

But of course the indeterminate fear is the most ir-
removable fear, so the child says, "I know, but I'm still
scared."

The mother does not answer the fright of the child.
A wise mother says, "Don't be frightened, I'm here."
That's not an answer to the child's fear, but it is a reply.

To the problem of evil there is, I think, no answer. But
there are replies.

There are really two parts to the problem of evil. First is its very existence. Upon that, I think we can throw a little, but not a thoroughly illuminating, light. The second part of the problem of evil is the absurdity of its distribution.

In his poem "Spring," Gerard Manley Hopkins speaks of "A strain of the earth's sweet being in the beginning." Hopkins talks of earth's beginning: the structure of all things as being under strain. There is built into the creation not a collapsed potential but an interior strain by virtue of which every potential has to move toward absolute realization or some form of actualization only by overcoming the difficulty of existence within the strain.

There can be no human good without the good having exercised choice, having confronted the possibility of that which is not good and by resolution, by insight, by courage, by will, having determined that the good shall be chosen and the evil shall be overcome. The very structure whereby the good comes into existence requires that there be a negativity which is the theater of the realization of the positive.

The word *beautiful* would be vacated of any meaning if the opposite—the unbecoming, the unbeautiful, the ugly—were not possible. It is not possible that anything like strength could be developed if strength did not have to exercise muscularity and discipline. In the midst of that which was opposed is the weak. So that there is a little light to be thrown upon the enigmatic statement, "I make weal and create woe, I am the Lord." This may mean that the precondition for the emergence of that which is good involves choice, freedom, resolution, decision, and discipline. Tautness is the precondition of harmony. There is a sense in which the evil, while not of the will of God, is a necessary component in the will to the good, the will to the unfolding and the maturation of that which shall be ever more fully human.

Of course, this little bit of light is no comfort to the person who is caught in the grip of evil, which, in most cases, is not a result of one's lack of resolution or having made a wrong choice. The long gray lines of people on their mordant way to annihilation in the Holocaust would not have been comforted by these thoughts. One thinks of the millions of people of all faiths or no faith who are overcome and done in and utterly ruined by events that were not of their own making, who have beat their fists against the indeterminacy of the problem of evil with full human passion.

We confront the bitter center of this problem when we ask about its second part: "Why the strange distribution of evil?" If evil were always justly distributed—that is, if the obstruction, that which must be overcome, were distributed in just relationship to the nature of a person's life or circumstances or character or potential—then some sense could be made of the distribution. But here there is absolute nonsense. Why is it that the prosperous, the strong, the aggressive, the cleverly calculating seem to get on very well and so many times the poor, the modest, the gentle seem to suffer under the forces of evil?

To the problem of the distribution of evil there is no answer, nor do I conceive of any possible way of stating the problem in which an answer could be clear or certain. But we can look to traditions and find the recorded rhetoric of the divine reply to the distribution of evil. The Old Testament singer says, "Even though I walk through the valley of the shadow of death, I fear no evil; for thou art with me" (Ps. 23:4), speaking of the God of Abraham, Isaac, and Jacob.

We have here a man who postulates no answer to the problem of death, which is ultimate evil. We have no answer to the problem, but we do have a reply that enables him to take, to contain, and to sustain faith in the midst of the valley of the shadow.

In the New Testament there is the awesome moment in which the death of Jesus Christ is recorded, particularly in the Gospel of Mark, with almost traumatic brevity and staccato language, when our Lord himself cried out, "My God, why hast thou forsaken me?" In the absence of a response, Jesus cries, "Into thy hands I commend my spirit." This word of trust, this handing over of oneself in trust in the midst of an absolute indeterminacy, is what I want to point out as a possible reply— not an answer to the problem of evil as a whole, but a reply out of the midst of evil.

Ever since the Second World War, there has become obvious in the United States an ever-deepening bewilderment as to the reality of the good, the strength and the persistence of the good: a coarsening of public sensibility toward the problems of personal and national morality, a coarsening of the public hide, as it were. The disastrous war in Vietnam, and the disclosures of the ambiguous character of those in charge of the highest public offices in our land have added to the deepening of moral sensibility that was invited and demanded by the Holocaust, but that has not commonly produced a group of persons in America who are probing with the relentlessness that we ought into the nature of our human responsibility in reply to the existence of evil.

In the face of these developments, what demands are made upon Christian and Jewish reflection? I don't mean only moral and temperamental demands upon the conscience, but I mean also intellectual and theological demands. First I want to discuss the law. I am a Lutheran, but I think I've come to think of this matter in an unconventional—and unconventionally Lutheran—way during the course of my adult life.

Lutheran theology has often misinterpreted the understanding of the law for the Jewish community. Ever since I was a child and used to listen to my father read in church from the Old Testament, I have wondered why the Christian community has failed to enter into the sense the Jewish community has for the meaning of Torah, the law. When I hear the normal Lutheran sermon stating, "We are the people who stand under the gospel, and thank God we do not stand under the law," I always find this difficult to understand, because I could not forget the resounding sentences I had heard my father read and still myself read from the Hebrew Scriptures: "Oh how I love thy law! It is my meditation all the day" (Ps. 119:97). The rhetoric of praise, of adoration, of appreciation, of the blessedness of the law in the Old Testament remains simply incomprehensible under our conventional Christian understanding.

How do we understand it properly? First, our English term *law* is by no means a big enough term to encompass what in the Hebrew language is meant by Torah—the God-given fundamental structures of creation. The Jew understands by the law the structure of fecundity, of proportion, of interrelationship, of guidance and stability which God gives and which comes to his people as instruction.

There is a reason why St. Paul talks about the law as being annihilated, as it were, by the coming of the good news of the grace and mercy of God and Jesus Christ, but Paul is not talking there about the whole compass and meaning and career of Torah. He was a child of a particular tradition, one that even Judaism knows to be only part of its full tradition and not by any means the amplest part.

Paul was a child of legalistic tradition in the late Judaism of his time, and therefore, he often talks about the law in a way that would seem not only to do no proper appreciative credit to what I've understood as the law in the Old Testament, but also to permit him to say that the law is absolutely repudiated, annihilated, is of no account in view of the gospel.

On the other hand, Paul knew too much about that aspect of the law that he does not refer to; he knew too much about it to permit him to go the whole way. Therefore, he catches himself time and time again and asks, "Has God forgotten his ancient people? Has God gone back on his promise to Abraham's people?" Then he uses in Greek what is very properly translated "God forbid," "It's an inadmissible thought" (*me genoito*). Therefore, Paul, as it were, talks out of both sides of his mouth, and we've heard only one part of it. How important is this?

It means that if we are going to enter into a fundamental discussion with the people of the covenant, God's ancient people of promise, we have got to move beyond the conventional modes of thought that have characterized both Catholic and Protestant theology. We've got to come under the amplitude of Jewish testimony to the meaning of the law and the moral vivacity, instruction, and ordering function of the law in the structure of human life and religious obedience to God.

This matter of the law, the Christian community's reopening of our whole relation via the Pauline literature in the New Testament to the law and the gospel to bring them together in a fresh way, is a prior item in future discussions between the Christian and the Jewish communities. One could put it as an epigram by saying, "Both the Jew and the Christian are related to the God of our fathers and the Father of our Lord Jesus Christ. We live reconciled to and accepted by him by grace."

*Hesed* and *hen* in the Old Testament are usually *charis* in the New Testament. But by virtue of that grace, we are not detached from our knowledge of and obedience to the fundamental structures of creation, and therefore we live under law and within grace at one and the same time. An interpretation of grace that does not understand the fundamental structures of creation as the theater for the actualization of life and grace is sloppy thinking.

Further, we have got to talk about the meaning of Christology for the Jewish community. There is no future in Christians trying to be more Christocentric than Jesus was. And Jesus was not Christocentric at all. His whole life, his words, actions, disposition, and final act were radically theocentric: "The one who sends me is the Father; the word that I speak is the word of the Father." That whole enormous momentum of the reality of God and the community of faith in God was his fabric and his context. In Christian understanding, Jesus is the incomparable and incandescent concreteness of the will and the word and the heart and the disposition of the God of Abraham, Isaac, and Jacob, who was his Father.

Without diminishing the enormous tradition in which one tries to clarify the intention and meaning and teaching and passional act of Jesus, without diminishing by one whit the importance, even the centrality, of that for Christian thought, the way is open to speak of the relation of the God of Abraham, Isaac, and Jacob, and the

God of our Lord Jesus Christ in a way in which Christology can fulfill its obligation toward the person and work of Christ without creating an absolute separation between the intentionality and the momentum of Judaism in its own God relationship.

When the apostle addressed the people of the Colossian congregation, having sharply reminded them in the early part of the letter about both their faith and their obligation, he used the interesting phrase, "redeeming the time" (Col. 4:5 KJV). Now to know what in one's time one ought to make an effort to redeem depends on what one finds damnation to be. Redemption is a meaningful possibility only in the presence of damnation.

I am not altogether sure that there is an absolutely clear, moral way to respond to many of the issues of our time. But I am absolutely clear that there is such a massive damnation existing in our time that if the church does not think and act on it, we will call down rightful judgment on ourselves. For the first time in mortal history we have the opportunity to annihilate God's earthly creation.

As I think of what I ought to do to be of some use in redeeming this time from the stalking damnation represented by nuclear arms, the following scenario leaps out at me and raps me sharply out of my lassitude. I imagine that there might be a time when one of my not-yet-incinerated grandchildren would put the question, "Grandfather, what were you doing when all this was a-gathering?" How awful it would be if I were to say that I spent my time simply talking about God.

# CHAPTER TEN

# Moral Discourse in a Nuclear Age

In each succeeding generation ethical issues demand ever deeper insight. Our parents knew as well as we that the Christian obligation is to hear the will of God and do it. In most instances they could find laws, biblical precedents, comparable instances and analogies whereby to guide their steps. They could ask with a certain admirable directness, "What does the Word of God teach concerning these matters?" We must ask the same question, but we cannot with equal clarity discern a guiding counsel for many problems of our time. Neither Scripture nor the body of Christian tradition can be transposed with adequate clarity into the tangled web of contemporary life. Fresh approaches are needed.

A dramatic instance of this need is the issue of death and dying. Contemporary medical knowledge makes possible the deferral of death by various means. The circumstances created within a family by the critical illness of a member are both clear and pathetic. The other members wish to obey the will of God, and they look to both Scripture and church tradition to furnish them with guidance, but neither Scripture nor tradition knows about the techniques of contemporary biological science and medical technology. Neither unambiguously tells us what we ought to do about genetically damaged fetuses, or what decision to make about continuing treatment for terminally ill grandparents. Faced with such situations, we are required to make absolute decisions between absolute options ("to live or let die"), and these absolutes must be obeyed within absolute indeterminacy.

The parables of Jesus have been critically established as being the closest we can possibly come to the eventful reality of Jesus himself—what he intended, what he purposed, what he determined to say and to be. Most of the parables begin, "Now the kingdom of God is like . . . ," or "The kingdom of God is as if. . . ." This opening is followed by a narrative. These narratives—often understood as illustrations, exemplary stories, or moral lessons—have through the centuries exuded inexhaustible invitations to reflection and even bewilderment. Their boundless vitality is the secret of their allure and the threat of their judgment. They are not, as we might wish, "perfectly clear." They invite trouble, they judge, and they promise; and they do all this with a continuing energy and pointedness that grasp us in every situation.

The parables of the kingdom are a kind of surgical exploration of those modes and postures of sin that blind, corrupt, and pervert humanity's relationship to God. Unless our Christian moral discourse permits the power of the parables to question and then correct that central perversion, we will continue to regard them merely as interesting illustrations, and in the process, pull the teeth of their intention. For they all say that the absolute permeation of our human condition by the power of sin, which all of us are loath to acknowledge, is the only acknowledgment whereby our redemption can be envisioned and received. The parables shock the mind into opening to the unenvisioned possible; they madly exaggerate in order to jolt the consciousness of the religiously secure; they are an assault upon the obvious. The entire momentum of conventional piety is brought into question: the man sells everything for the one thing; the shepherd leaves the 99 undefended in order to find the lost one; in defiance of common sense, the woman takes the house apart to find the lost coin; the lord commends the unjust steward for his uncanny perception of the truth. Is it not possible that the accounts of the miracles are enacted forms of the parables? The parables are spoken miracles; the miracles are enacted parables.

Inasmuch as the people of God strive to discern God's will in every situation and to pray for the gifts of grace to receive it, and inasmuch as Jesus most succinctly speaks of this will of God in the parables, may it not follow that a Christian mode of ethical discourse might be most fruitfully suggested by a never-ending attention to these parables? This way of inquiry is particularly apposite as the church probes for a proper response to the immensely complex issues of peacemaking and peacekeeping. For here the question of right obedience mirrors on a huge scale precisely the tormenting problems we confront on a small scale when we ask the bedside question, "To live or let die?"

To illustrate more concretely what may be suggested by the term "fresh modes of moral reflection," we may bring under scrutiny several terms central to the politics of living in a nuclear age, terms that occur in every sober discussion of peacekeeping.

It is alleged that deterrence, guaranteed threats of unacceptable harm between conflicting nation-states, averts actual warfare between the superpowers, diverting attention to other means of resolving conflicts. Deterrence is seen as holding in check the violent impulses on both sides. This term has achieved a strange reputation for cool rationality. Our confidence in the idea and the policy of deterrence is soberly maintained against all the evidence to the contrary. For in fact, deterrence does not deter. The madness of trying to avert death by the multiplication of its means only evokes ongoing escalations of the arms race. Power, believed to be a deterrent, always invites the development of a more threatening counterpower. The invention of the stirrup gave mounted warriors greater strength; the fabrication of armor was the rejoinder. Big guns could sink wooden ships; iron plates were the rejoinder. The machine gun multiplied fire power; tanks were invented. Aircraft begot antiaircraft. Big bombs became the superbombs dropped on Hiroshima. Moral generalities are hazardous, but this one is clear: angry and prideful people will envision, devise, and use whatever will destroy the enemy. There is no ground for confidence that current speculations about extending our earthly obscenities to the heavens would accomplish anything but an equivalent rejoinder, and thus infect with our evil the unoffending stars.

The uncritical acceptance of the self-deception implied in the term *deterrence* and the clear history of the failure of such a policy suggest that the terms *irrational* and *unrealistic*, which are often used with Olympian confidence to dismiss all who would suggest radically new possibilities for human communities, have lost all *ra-tional* meaning. In fact, a strange and parabolic reversal has occurred in our time. Until recently, notes Paul G. Johnson in a *Christian Century* article ("The Bifocaled Lutheran Vision of Peace," December 21-28, 1983, p. 1178), it has been the "dreamers" and "idealists" who opposed war and held out visions for a peaceful world, and the "realists" who accepted war as tragically inevitable for the human species. Now, writes Johnson, the tables have been turned. It has become the starkest "realism" to acknowledge that the world will be blown up if we do nothing to stop nuclear madness, and the thinnest "dream" to suppose that anything short of nuclear disarmament can avert this catastrophe. If two angry persons were to confront each other with weapons of mutually assured destruction, and if one of them were a so-called utopian dreamer who mused that "there must be some other way . . . ," the term *rational* might more becomingly be used of the dreamer than of the opposing *realist*.

The possibility here for a fresh mode of moral reflection is exactly like that which haunts us in the parables of Jesus. In those stories the new, the possible, the mad reversal of our expectations constitute the enduring promise and mind-tormenting power of the biblical Word. Such theological pondering of the Word is methodologically more appropriate than the proof-text snippets marshaled as evidence to nail down conventional moralities. In the words of W. H. Auden's "Christmas Oratorio," *For the Time Being*, "Nothing can save us that is possible. We who are about to die demand a miracle."

Deterrence also implies that the other side is evil and cannot be trusted, whereas our side is good. To postulate a dichotomy that sees the evil as primarily the character of the *other* is the sly and fateful way our self-deception operates. Evil is never more quietly powerful than in the assumption that it resides elsewhere. The term "evil empire" is a description of all empires. The internal empire of every person's egocentricity is the template of historical evil.

The word *verification* is currently used to say that if I make a contract with my neighbor to follow agreed-upon procedures, that contract must be secured by our mutual ability empirically to check compliance. In such a contract the term is clear and the necessity obvious. When, however, the term is transferred to the realm of moral discourse, the adjective *moral* both indicates and describes a radically new context. That context both presupposes and requires that the element of trust decisively modify the spirit as well as the expectations of the conferring persons.

What I cannot trust I must verify. But if I must verify in order to converse, I have not a conversation but a purely calculated negotiation in which every possibility for movement is annihilated by the minutiae of tit-for-tat. All genuine trust implies risk. All human relations go beyond the verifiable, and unspokenly assume that the hopes, the needs, the longings of the other are not utterly discontinuous with one's own. Indeed, my own self-interest demands and is commonly characterized by such an assumption. I do not verify my physician's statement that the treatment he prescribes is based on his scientific reading of the data, or question that his professional self-interest is on the side of telling the truth. In an even more fundamental relationship, a man and a woman do not verify their conjugal promises, nor insist on verification in every aspect of their relationship. They trust one another. It is not here suggested that trust can replace the conventions of treaty obligations in pacts between nations, but it is suggested that even within such transindividual relationships, the assumption of the continuities of elemental human desires, fears, and visions of a better world does exist and operate. At the very least the rigidity of our stereotypes of other nations must be modified by the sheer dynamism of historical change. Should we continue to deal with the U.S.S.R. as if Stalin were still the boss?

In the very considerable literature on peace and politics, the term *peace* is commonly used as if it referred to a disengaged and highly desirable virtue, achievement, or gift hanging in splendid and beguiling isolation. Such an assumption oversimplifies. It suggests the notion of an exclusively interior and private serenity, a well-insulated tranquility achieved by detachment. By *peace* the devout often mean the bovine contentment sustained only by a virtual ignorance or dismissal of all that maddens, saddens, and gladdens the generality of humankind.

Among Christians, *peace* dare not be used in this antiseptic way. The peace of God is more profound. In the Scriptures, peace has meanings so many and various that they cannot be condensed into a single statement; all such meanings operate within a context, and that context always involves discipline, choices, denials, sacrifices.

These choices can be illustrated by scrutinizing our motives and those of our fellows as we inquire why we want peace. When, not long ago, I saw a group of women from a wealthy suburb of my city marching in a peace rally and observed the elegance of their expensive attire, their Gucci shoes, and the waiting chauffeur-driven cars

at the edge of the square, I could not but recall the statement of a wise man: "Everybody wants peace. But we
also want what we cannot have without war." We all
want to sustain the standard of living we have become
accustomed to. We all want our proud nation to be number one. We all want to maintain access to minerals and
fuels, no matter where located, that are the necessary
components of our technologically advanced society. In
other words, though we all want peace, we also want
one system or another that allows the fulfillment of our
wishes, wants, and delights to continue unabated. We
want our peace. But the peace that God wills cannot be
given when we understand peace only in egocentric
terms. The power of the strong to control what they
want evokes an outcry from the weak.

Throughout the Scriptures, love, righteousness, and
justice are a trinity of terms that swirl around and penetrate each other. In one passage or another, each may
have a primary reference, but its context almost always
pushes out to enlarge its meaning through reference to
the others. The righteousness of God is not separable
from his will to reconcile all creation to himself, and that
reconciliation presupposes love and justice. The works
of love are never specified apart from the obligation to
regard and deal with the other with justice.

The coexistence and interplay of these terms is illuminating when, as in our present inquiry into "peace
and politics," we properly place strong emphasis on the
power of love. What is the nature of this love that
throughout the Scriptures is affirmed to be fundamental
to the nature of God himself? A barrier to a comprehensive understanding of love is our attempt to grasp
the fullness of its meaning by comparing it to mutual

love in intimate personal relations. We grope for an adequate understanding from the perspective of our own purely individual and private experience of love.

But love is not merely an affection. Love's surplusage is disclosed when we puzzle over Jesus' statement, "A new commandment I give to you, that you love one another" (John 13:34). That love is commanded is puzzling. As we clearly know, love cannot be commanded. It emerges, occurs—we "fall in love." There is something incomprehensible in all instances of our human love. But Jesus nevertheless commands it. What kind of love is this?

I am not told that I am to *like* my neighbor; I am ordered to *love* him or her. Luther's explication of our relation to the neighbor brings us close to a right understanding. Our neighbors, in the biblical sense, are those persons who live in God's creation with us in the solidarity of our life together on this earth. Though I cannot will myself to feel an oceanic affection for all people, I can acknowledge my bond with the whole of creation. In that bond I am to recognize the authenticity, the *thereness*, the concrete life and existence of the other.

In the broad context of human solidarity the exercise of love is realized in transaffectional justice. Real love grasps the hand that need holds out. Needs cry out from millions I will never meet. Justice is love operating at a distance. When, for instance, my church tells me that millions of people are starving and that it is my duty to show my love for them through helpful actions, I become aware of the transindividual meaning of love. I cannot feel any immediate affection for two million people. Love becomes a recognition of the neighbor in his or her need, and takes the transpersonal form of distributed food.

Just as love is transposed into acknowledgment, and hence can be commanded, so the term *justice* can be opened up when pondered in continuity with this commanded love. Even in pre-Christian and non-Christian discourse, the term *justice* affirms people's solidarity within a shared theater of existence that absolutely requires order, limit, and the acknowledgment of rights. Justice is not an invented and imposed virtue; it is a precondition for human life. The Old Testament does not create the idea or the term. It presupposes that ordering and ascribes it to God the Creator. That order is an aspect of God's righteousness; its denial brings one under God's judgment. The prophets' vehemence and the cutting clarity of their judgment makes clear that injustice is blasphemy before the holy, not just failure before the civil.

Consequently, it is clear that any envisionment of peace that is purely interior and dispositional—as a kind of tranquil ambience for the inner life—is a disastrous reduction. It is equally clear that peace is impossible without transforming the meaning and exercise of love beyond its egocentric theater, and that any exercise of love that does not intersect and demand the primal human dignity and world-ordering called *justice* is futile.

## A Proposal

It is exactly the parables' cogency in giving us a vision of what a "fresh mode of moral discourse" might provide that suggests the following proposal. The genius of the parables is their insistence on the power of God's possible. The envisionment of the possible haunts the mind into the quest for fresh ways of dealing with the indeterminate character of our moral quandaries.

At present most churches have no continuing structure to deal with the kind of issues described here. As
issues arise and the demand for guidance becomes clamant, we assemble an ad hoc study. A different issue
convokes another conference. Would it not be possible
for each communion to establish an ongoing "Commission on Theology and Ethics"? Such a commission could
deepen and refine the continuing reflection of a community of conversation. It should include not only the
church's scholars, but also those nonacademic persons
whose intelligence, concern, sensibility, specialized
knowledge, and spiritual endowments might serve to
invite scholarship into the more ample and immediate
phenomena and language of the common life. An ad-
ditional virtue of such a commission would be its possibility for perceiving and specifying such fresh modes
of moral discourse as the circumstances require.

Twentieth-century modes of thought, life, and work
present us with new issues for moral reflection. Problems arising from advances in the biological sciences are
but one example of such emerging and pressing moral
issues. A continuing communal process of moral discourse would create a fermenting compost heap of reflection within which the modes of thought sharpened
by dealing with one issue could penetrate and illuminate
another.

# CHAPTER ELEVEN

# Aging: A Summing Up and a Letting Go

Aging has been called "an awkward problem." The dramatic growth in sheer numbers and in longevity of the world population has excited students from many disciplines—demographers, anthropologists, sociologists, psychologists, educators, politicians, philosophers, theologians, and all the specialists within the general category of medicine. An article in the *New England Journal of Medicine* ("Benefit and Cost Analysis in Geriatric Care" by Jerry Avorn, M.D., May 17, 1984) describes and critically analyzes the three major proposals for dealing with the problem of how most justly to relate health resources to fresh circumstances. An interesting paragraph near the end of that essay provides me with an appropriate entrance into the issue I want to discuss here. "Little comfort can be found in the standard argument that decisions on resource allocation are made on the basis of 'gut feelings' all the time, and that

these methods are an improvement over such impreci-
sion. Approximate as gut feelings may be, they remain
superior to delusional systems, no matter how detailed
they are."

The capacious phrase "gut feelings" seeks to scoop
up all the phenomena of aging that slip through the
technological grid of the method that informs all the
proposals so carefully described. That method is em-
pirical, demographic-statistical, rich in elaboration of
physical data. It is a method that, since Descartes, has
achieved an almost absolute dominance as a way to
study and envision programs for the solutions of all human problems. The arrogance with which this method
is calmly applied is, of course, sustained with slight embarrassment by its massive success since the days of the
Enlightenment. The submersion of qualitative realities
into the heady solution of quantitative methods has in
our time reached the state for which Hannah Arendt's
term *banality* is alone adequate. It is inevitable that the
exercise of this method in the determination of models
for health care for the aging should elevate the term
*productivity* to normative status. Productivity thus conceived is really equivalent to worth. Indeed, this essay
boldly identifies personal worth with the kind of productivity that can be specified in dollar value. This
strange calculus is not only offensive to moral sensibility;
it represents so radical a compression of a large term as
also to offend common sense. John Keats, in utter pov-
erty and fatally ill the last two years of his short life,
composed in those few months the odes which secure
his place among the great poets.

So we return to the question. Why is aging an *awkward*
problem? The term is commonly used to designate aspects of a situation for which conventional modes are

felt wanting, circumstances for which usual procedures are inappropriate. We sometimes use the word *awkward* to describe a social or interpersonal situation in which the unexpected upsets the anticipated. The fact that human life has a limit, that life moves inexorably toward death, is to the common mind of a technically informed culture of the West an awkward fact, for our entire educational system is geared to the transmission of problem-solving techniques and devices. Popular culture is invited to assume that knowledge, resolution, time, and an adequate allocation of funds can solve all problems. A branch of the American armed forces in the Second World War invented an interesting maxim: "The difficult we do at once; the impossible takes a little longer." Professor Hans Jonas once wrote an essay in which he mused over the disposition of our generation to regard death as an awkward interruption of a play that was so pleasantly getting on very well. Human life has been increasingly brought under such managerial powers as to make death a cheat, a ludicrous interruption, an event for which an entire profession has conspired to cosmetize the dead and narcotize the survivors.

No brief essay can designate or adequately describe those interior dimensions of aging to which I have alluded as determining the awkwardness that inheres in the methodological models. But some of these may be pointed to and given a voice. On the assumption that the memorable literature of the human family is the most enduring confessional of human inwardness, I have for several years been collecting such expressions. I am astonished at the plenitude, the force, the variety, and the eloquence of these sentences. From Homer to the literature of our present moment, the huge mass is richly strewn with the reality of aging giving voice to a ductile, but awesome and universal, interior truth that is not capable of quantification. The most deeply human is not amenable to digital reduction.

Several themes are central, pervasive, and many-voiced. The fundamental feeling that colors the affective life of all of us who are at or beyond the biblical "three score and ten" can best be designated by the term *pathos*. Pathos is not a simple thing; it is an ever-more acute sense of passingness, of the urgency of unretrievable time, the knowledge that time leans forward, a sense that the recurring events of life have a limit—this place I may not see again, this one I may never greet again, this little company around the table may never again around another table meet. The interior sensibility of aging is made pathetic by a radical elimination of all those relationships and components that have consti-tuted one's life world. John Donne's "Every man's death diminishes me" leaps from formal fact to individual ex-perience with terrifying force. The network of personal relationships constitutes the interior tonality of a life, and the fragility of these relationships is recognized in old age with particular hurt. The quiet departures within this personal world are snapped like filaments in the web of identity.

I know no statement of the pathos of the aging spirit more rich and true than the opening lines of William Shakespeare's Sonnet 73. The common image out of which these lines distill their beauty and velocity is the image of a springtime green tree alive with the voices of birds, and that same tree against a sullen, autumnal sky when October shall have come again.

> *That time of year thou mayst in me behold*
> *When yellow leaves, or none, or few, do hang*

*Upon those boughs which shake against the cold,*
*Bare ruin'd choirs where late the sweet birds sang.*

These lines are not the statement of a problem await-
ing solution; they are, rather, a statement of the human
condition for which there is no solution. The demand
is, rather, for courage, acquiescence, resignation, acceptance—some coming to terms with. They are a time
of remembering, gathering up and sorting out, discrim-
inating between the abiding and the evanescent, a time
of perhaps unmarked passage from knowledge to wisdom, from simple awareness to insight, to what Jona-
than Edwards called "consent to being," to the psalmist's
"so teach us to number our days that we may get a heart
of wisdom," a movement of the total spirit from an anx-
ious hanging-on to a graceful letting-be, a releasement.

If this were an essay of another sort I could elaborate
my own transaction within this awkwardness. But the
purpose of this short piece is rather a transpersonal one:
to state a problem in terms appropriate to its universality
and its profundity, and thus to suggest that discussions
of health and medicine achieve a wise sense of humor
whereby to modify their often brusque proposals.

When I was in my first parish in Cleveland, I spent
some time with Walter Holtcamp, Melville
Smith, and others at the Holtcamp Shop, which was
creating the first American Baroque organ. I learned
something about organ building and voicing, and I
helped install the first Baroque pipe organ in America
in the Cleveland Museum of Art. I turned the pages for

Albert Schweitzer when he inaugurated it with the Franck "Chorale in A Minor."

I spoke with Walter Holtcamp Jr. recently about those early days when organ builders sought above everything to get clarity in the organ tone so that there wasn't a big sonorous romantic mush but clear voices to articulate the polyphonic music of the period of Bach and Buxtehude. "Well," he said, "I've got news for you! They don't even want clarity anymore. The new generation *wants* mush. The more romantic and mushy you can make it, the better they like it."

This evoked a deep sadness in me, but I won't try to understand it. The older I get, the fewer things I understand. Some of you may have heard of the response from a famous literary figure who, upon the acceptance of a prestigious award near the end of his life, was asked to make a brief statement. He said: "I'm an old man; it's a strange world; I don't understand a damn thing." The older I get the more sympathy I have with this sentiment.

*

Old age is a time of gathering diminishments. The maturation of hope and expectation into experience reverses in aging. There is literally no future. All the little filaments of personal relations that constitute your world snap loose, one after another.

I think of the world in which I was an active teacher and churchman and worker. Ted Tappard, Franklin Fry, Paul Krouse, Willem Visser 't Hooft—all that company of world theologians of which I was not a peer, but a little guy among the greats—Reinhold and Richard Niebuhr, Rudolf Bultmann, Karl Barth, and Emil Brunner—I knew the whole bunch! We were on the World

Council of Churches' Faith and Order Commission together. For 30 years of my life I was a member of the
group I now sardonically remember called itself "the
younger theologians." We met twice a year in the House
of Preachers at Washington Cathedral, because it was
offered to us and it was cheap. Other members of the
group were Henry Pitney Van Deusen, James Luther
Adams, Wilhelm Pauck, and Paul Tillich. Now Jim Adams and I are the only two left.

We respond with a combination of rejoicing and mel-
ancholy. One would think that to talk of aging in true
and realistic terms of diminishment, of passingness,
would be depressing to the aged. Take it from me, the
very opposite is the case. When I appear among my
peers—old people who ask me sometimes to come because they know my special interest in them—when I
come and give them bits of the literature on aging, which
I know by heart now and can recite to them, I find that
they both weep and are consoled, because they know
they are not alone. This is the human condition; this is
the company toward membership in which we all are
moving.

Heaven is a metaphor for the fulfillment of life in
God. I remember once I was interim pastor in a
congregation and a lady came to me, a nice lady who
had experienced a very fulfilling and wonderful mar-
riage. Her husband had died the autumn before, and
she was in deep grief. She said, "You know, it's particularly hard late in the afternoon sitting at the window
watching where he used to come around the corner in
summertime, his coat over his arm, slapping his leg with

the evening paper. He always stopped just when he thought I couldn't see him and knocked out his pipe. He knew I didn't want him to smoke so much, although I kept sewing up the burnt holes in his coat pockets. That time of day is a terrible one for me to get through, because I know he won't come around the corner any more. In heaven do you suppose he and I will live together in a cottage with a white fence?"

This was pathetic. I appreciate the woman's grief and affection, but I can't say, "Yes, yes, in heaven that's the way it's going to be." That would be a lie. Who would manufacture the old shag tobacco in heaven? There would have to be a pipe-making shop and a tweed jacket to carry the pipe in. That is simply not true to the Christian faith.

*

We must stop this conspiracy of silence about death, and talk openly about it. One can go to church a whole lifetime and never hear a sermon on death.

If I were a young preacher again, I would preach the Christian gospel of eternal life in God, but I would preach it sooner in my ministry, preach it throughout, and I would preach it more realistically. The Bible really has nothing to say about eternal life. That sounds like a shocking statement, but it's literally true: there is not a single clear and concrete word in the Bible about life after death. It affirms that life with God is life with that which does not die. But any specification about life after death is steadily avoided by the biblical writers.

Paul made an effort to address the question, but it's a bum effort: "What you sow does not come to life unless it dies. And what you sow is not the body which is to be, but a bare kernel, perhaps of wheat or of some other grain. But God gives it a body as he has chosen, and to each kind of seed its own body. For not all flesh is alike, but there is one kind for men, another for animals, another for birds, and another for fish" (1 Cor. 15:36-39). He tries by natural analogy to say something. Interestingly, he never tried it again.

In Romans, the most mature of Paul's epistles, he says, "If we live, we live to the Lord, and if we die, we die to the Lord; so then, whether we live or whether we die, we are the Lord's" (Rom. 14:8). Period! That is the fundamental and absolute word of Scripture. But that word is immensely satisfying to old people. I never try to give any blueprints of eternity or heaven or eternal life, since by definition it is utterly impossible.

I think instead of trying to answer all the questions about death, we ought to follow the example of Paul and the New Testament and say, "Eye has not seen nor ear heard"; "By faith we are saved."

By faith we are saved.